May the God who is both great and good
make your marriage stronger and your hearts braver.
May He create not only a willingness to die for your
marriage but also a passion to live for it.

What people are saying about ...

SOULgasm:
CARING FOR YOUR SOUL AND THE
SOUL OF YOUR MARRIAGE

✢ Biblical, practical and wise, SOUL*gasm* is a 'soup-to-nuts' guide to the spiritual vitality of individuals and their marriage. Readers, single and married, will appreciate how the book exposes not only common sinkholes to spiritual health but also surprising pathways of spiritual renewal. In attending to the health of our souls, as individuals and as a one-flesh union of marriage, SOUL*gasm* grows stronger marriages and fills a gap in the Christian literature on marriage. Thank you, Anne+Tim Evans!

Mimi Haddad, PhD., President, CBE
International www.cbeinternational.org

✢ With a wealth of wisdom and a depth of experience, Tim and Anne encourage, inspire, and challenge couples to a deeper level of intimacy and enjoyment with God and with each other. Not only do they equip you with practical steps but they lead by example. Their marriage is a beautiful picture of what it means to truly *enjoy and delight* in the gift of marriage.

Debra Fileta, M.A., LPC author of *Choosing Marriage* and creator of relationship advice blog TrueLoveDates.com

✢ Anne+Tim have many tools they use in counseling and ministering to couples. Now they are sharing them in an easy-to-read book that invites couples to grow in intimacy and experience SOUL*gasm*. Reading the book felt like we were having an extended visit that was filled with wisdom, insightful conversation, laughter, and many "AHA" moments. No matter where you are in your marriage, this book is a must-read.

Terri + Jack Brown, lead pastors of *The Table Church*, Colorado Springs, Colorado

✛ Although those who marry will "experience troubles in this life," it is in and through those difficulties that the greatest possibility for transformational intimacy occurs. In this book, Anne+Tim challenge marrieds, young and old, to enjoy, relish, and embrace this God-designed and Spirit-directed journey—*together*. As the authors share spiritual truths by weaving them into their own stories of relational success and failure, they shed light on the path toward more moments of spiritual ecstasy. The more they shared, the more I became wholeheartedly convinced that "I need more; I need more SOUL*gasm* in my marriage." You will too!

Rev. Sue Bailey, founder of look4god. com, pastor, teacher, speaker, mentor, and coordinator of CBE Denver Chapter

✛ This book is a roadmap that will transform your marriage into a masterpiece. While many marriages lack fulfillment, Tim+Anne have provided the tools to move from the status quo—to intimacy—to experiencing SOUL*gasm*. We highly recommend this book for anyone who desires all God has designed for marriage.

Jacob + Hannah Ouellette, lead pastors of *Thrive Church*, Parker, Colorado

✛ Tim+Anne are the most real people I know. Reading SOUL*gasm* was an invitation to better know this couple who have lived out marriage in a genuine and authentic fashion for over forty years. Anne+Tim's marriage journey has been a powerful model worth learning about. I appreciate their integrative approach to matters of oneness in a way that honors God. As you read SOUL*gasm,* you will be enriched, challenged, and refreshed with a new appreciation for how your spirit, soul, and body are designed and intertwined for deep intimacy—and experiencing SOUL*gasm*.

Wilmer Villacorta, PhD., Associate professor, School of Intercultural Studies (MAGL), Fuller Theological Seminary

NOUN, VERB/
SOL-GÁ-ZAM
An emotional response to ordinary and extra-ordinary MOMENTS A SURGE OF delight a Gentle wash of POSITIVITY ECSTASY

LIFE-giving JOY

SOULgasm

Caring for Your **Soul** and the **Soul** of Your Marriage

NOUN, VERB/
SOL-GA-ZAM
An
emotional
response to
ordinary
and extra-
ordinary
MOMENTS
A
SURGE OF
delight
a
Gentle
wash of
POSITIVITY
ECSTASY

LIFE-
giving
JOY

SOUL*gasm*

Caring for Your **Soul** and the **Soul** of Your Marriage

anne+tim evans

SOUL*gasm*: Caring for Your Soul and the Soul of Your Marriage

Published by REAL LIFE Ministries

PO Box 6800, Colorado Springs, CO 80934

For ordering information visit Amazon.com

All Scripture quotations, unless otherwise noted, are taken from the New American Standard Bible®, Copyright © 1960, 1995 by The Lockman Foundation. Used by permission. (www.Lockman.org.)

Scripture quotations marked "ESV" are taken from the ESV® Bible (The Holy Bible, English Standard Version®) copyright © 2001 by Crossway, a publishing ministry of Good News Publishers. ESV® Text Edition: 2011. The ESV® text has been reproduced in cooperation with and by permission of Good News Publishers. Unauthorized reproduction of this publication is prohibited. All rights reserved. Scripture quotations marked "NIV" are taken from the Holy Bible, New International Version®, NIV®. Copyright © 1973, 1984 by Biblica, Inc.™ Used by permission of Zondervan. All rights reserved worldwide. www.zondervan.com. Scripture quotations marked "KJV" are from the King James Version (Public Domain). Scripture quotations marked "NKJV" are taken from the New King James Version®. Copyright © 1982 by Thomas Nelson. Used by permission. All rights reserved. Scripture quotations marked "NLT" are taken from the *Holy Bible,* New Living Translation, copyright © 1996, 2004, 2015 by Tyndale House Foundation. Used by permission of Tyndale House Publishers Inc., Carol Stream, IL 60188. All rights reserved. Scripture quotations marked "TLB" are from the Living Bible, copyright © 1971 by Tyndale House Foundation. Used by permission of Tyndale House Publishers Inc., Carol Stream, IL 60188. All rights reserved. The Living Bible, TLB, and The Living Bible logo are registered trademarks of Tyndale House Publishers.

The authors have added italics to Scripture quotations for emphasis.

ISBN 978-0-578-20928-9

© 2018 Anne and Tim Evans

Cover design; Susan Murdock, Beryl Glass, Amy Deboer, and Kathleen White

Printed in the United States of America

First Edition 2018

DEDICATION

We dedicate SOUL*gasm* to couples who passionately
pursue God's creational marriage design; and
who take ownership and responsibility to care
for their souls, and the soul of their marriage.

CONTENTS

+ PART THREE - SOUL*GASM* NEXT STEPS

NOTES TO READERS

+ *Anne + Tim (we) write from a traditional, Judeo-Christian, orthodox marriage perspective. Our desire is to offer for your consideration marriage views based on over forty years of marriage, decades of counseling experiences, and a number of Bible passages as we currently understand them. However, we recognize and respect that people have a wide range of beliefs, opinions, and feelings—especially surrounding marriage, intimacy, and sexuality.*

+ *Names and details regarding many individuals whose stories are told in this book have been changed to protect their privacy. Editorial liberties have been taken to combine certain people, stories, and circumstances for the purpose of clarity and illustration. In addition, certain portions are reprinted from our REAL LIFE MARRIAGE, TOGETHER or NAKED books.*

+ *A note to unmarried readers: The main focus of this book is for Christian married couples. However, we believe unmarried readers will also benefit from reading it as they grow in understanding God's creational marriage design. Always remember that God created every person (single and married) in His image. He gave every man and woman legitimate longings for intimacy and the desire to live life with passion. Furthermore, every single person's ability to experience SOULgasm can be enjoyed apart from being married. Remember, the apostle Paul, Mary Magdalene, and Jesus Christ were all unmarried and led pretty amazing lives. All that is to say, we welcome single readers, and we are grateful for the selfless ways you humbly walk out your love for God and others.*

+ *More than a decade ago when we began brainstorming about our REAL LIFE marriage book series, we knew one of our books would focus on God's creational marriage design and co-leadership in marriage (see Appendix A). That led to co-authoring* TOGETHER: Reclaiming Co-Leadership in Marriage.[1] *Our next book focused on sexual intimacy—and God is pro-sex! This led to writing* NAKED: Reclaiming Sexual Intimacy in Marriage.[2] *This book,* SOULgasm: Caring for Your Soul and the Soul of Your Marriage, *focuses on the life-giving soul connection between a husband and wife. The kind of connection that makes a man and woman fall in love. The kind of connection that helps a husband and wife honor covenant for a lifetime. The kind of connection that invites them to keep coming back for more—until death parts them. In addition, all of these marriage books have* Companion Journals *for couples or groups to work through together.*

+ *Whenever we read a book, we like to know a little about the author. We suspect you may feel the same way. Therefore, you may be wondering, who are anne+tim evans? When describing ourselves, first and foremost we say that we are followers of Jesus Christ. Therefore, we purposefully place God at the center of our lives, marriage, family, ministry, relationships, and writing. We went to kindergarten together, had a crush on each other in middle school, got married at twenty-one, and have been married over forty years. We are a real-life couple—a retired fire chief and a nurse—who are parents, grandparents, spiritual parents, authors, and pastoral counselors. We live in Colorado Springs and co-lead REAL LIFE Ministries full time.*

WHY SHOULD YOU INVEST IN READING THIS BOOK?

The truth is that countless marriage books and resources are available. While working with couples, we've observed that they don't long for another "how-to" book, more marriage "dos and don'ts," or the latest marriage "tips-tools-techniques." Couples don't need an author's guaranteed promises of "a trouble-free marriage and epic intimacy." What we believe they do need is to include God in everything, understand their true identity, honor covenant, be kind and gracious to each other, take ownership and responsibility for their part in marriage, and embrace God's creational marriage design.

+ As we begin our authors/reader journey, we'd like to pray a prayer over every reader, "Lord, just like you opened the heart of Lydia, a worshipper of God, to respond to Paul's message,[3] please open the hearts of those who invest in reading this book. We pray every husband and wife advances in intimacy with God and with their spouse, and they grow in experiencing SOULgasm."

FOREWORD

"Each one of us hides an awful secret. Buried deep within every human soul throbs a muted pain that never goes away. It is a lifelong yearning for that one love that will never be found, the languishing in our inner selves for an all-consuming intensity of intimacy that we know will never be fulfilled, a heart-need to surrender all that we are to a bond that will never fail.

The silent churning at the core of our being is the tormenting need to know and to be known, to understand and to be understood, to possess and to be possessed, to belong unconditionally and forever without fear of loss, betrayal or rejection. It is the nostalgia for our primal oneness, the silent sorrowing for Paradise lost, the age-long pursuit after the encompassing embrace for which we know we were created. It is the search, however wanton and sullied, for the pristine grace of holding and being held, for the freedom to be who we really are without shame or pretense, for release and repose in the womb-like safety of unalterable acceptance and of overarching love."[1]

It took two decades after the publishing of these words that describe the human condition at its very core, for the book evocatively entitled SOUL*gasm* to appear. At last, the yearnings expressed in the quote above find their fulfillment in the pages of SOUL*gasm* as it prescribes the pursuit of "God's creational marriage principles, fiercely fighting for marriages and families, and passionately embracing mutuality and functional equality—which will result in seeing God's glory in couples' marriage stories."

Dr. Gilbert Bilezikian, cofounder of Willow Creek
Community Church and professor emeritus
at Wheaton College, Wheaton, Illinois

INTRODUCTION

SOUL*gasm* —we love that word. So much so that we thought it would make a great title for this third book in our REAL LIFE marriage series. As we considered using SOUL*gasm* for our book title, we took an informal survey to see what people thought. The question we asked was this: *What do you think about the word* SOUL*gasm for a book title?* We got some interesting responses. Some said the title piqued their curiosity enough to want to learn more. They told us that if they were in a bookstore and noticed a book on the shelf titled SOUL*gasm*, they would take it down and browse through the table of contents.

Others, who leaned more toward an editing bent (we refer to them as *word people*), responded to our question with a question. They asked, "SOUL *what*?" And there were others who struggled getting past the fact that SOUL*gasm* was not an official, dictionary-approved word. So we directed them to the *Urban Dictionary*, and we assured them our book would be adding to this definition:

> **SOUL*gasm***—noun, verb \sōl-ga-zəm\
> A moment of pure spiritual ecstasy; in which, an artful piece of life touches and moves the very core of your being, forcing you to close your eyes, gape slightly and lose yourself in its beauty, and as you do, a delightful ting-ling sensation flourishes from the back of your head and travels down your neck to ravish the entirety of your flesh.[1]

Okay, we understand the word SOUL*gasm* is not in *Webster's*, but whoever said every word a person uses has to be dictionary approved? There are plenty of great words just waiting to be discovered. For example, in a scene from the Christmas holiday movie *Elf*, Buddy was doubting his ability to be a toy maker. Do you remember the word he used to describe himself? He said he'd always be a "cottonheaded ninnymuggins." Now, no one needed to pull out the dictionary to try to figure out what Buddy meant. He made up a word that pretty much defined itself.

The last category of people who participated in our informal survey wondered if SOUL*gasm* had sexual connotations. They thought the title was sexual in nature and related to orgasm. We assured them the climax of excitement we write about in this book is centered in the SOUL and is emotional in nature.

Lastly, when we asked married couples what they thought about the title SOUL*gasm*, they said it reminded them of a way to describe the emotional connection—the soul oneness—God designed for a husband and wife. As we reviewed our book title survey, we discovered the vast majority of people liked the title. More specifically, they loved the way the word sounded—SOUL*gasm*.

As we continued our search for the title (okay, we didn't go as far as Buddy the elf and make up a crazy new word), we took the word SOUL and used it as our root word, and then we added a suffix. Just by tagging four simple letters—*g-a-s-m*—to the noun SOUL, it created the title we were searching for—SOUL*gasm*.

A next step after choosing the title was determining the illustration for the front cover of SOUL*gasm*. After input and processing, we decided to use a simple exclamation point — ! — which we believe emphasizes a SOUL*gasm* experience.

SO WHY GASM?

Stop and think about it—*gasm* can be used in countless ways to creatively describe an experience. For example, if you are a person who loves shoes and you find yourself in the middle of the shoe department, you may experience a SHOE*gasm*.

If you are a person who loves food (affectionately referred to as a *foodie*), and you find yourself surrounded by delicious cuisine, you may experience a FOOD*gasm*.

If you are someone who loves technology and are constantly thinking about things related to pixels, bytes, wikis, cookies, or RSS feeds, you may experience regular NERD*gasms*.

You get the idea, whatever kind of *gasm* you are enjoying, whether it's a SPORTS*gasm*, MIND*gasm*, MUSIC*gasm*, FILM*gasm*, ADVENTURE*gasm*, ART*gasm*—these are all associated with positive experiences that bring pleasure to the soul. They may vary in intensity and be a response to any number of things, but they include the kind of joyful pleasure that makes you want to come back for more.

Remember we said we would expand on the definition found in the *Urban Dictionary*? Well, simply put, SOUL*gasm* brings positive emotional pleasure to the soul. It's a human reaction that provides a variety of responses that vary in intensity. While SOUL*gasm* can be described as an intense surge of joy that pulses through the entire body, it can also be described as a gentle wash of tender emotions that are accompanied by tingling in a person's body and soul.

A SOULgasm is an internal response to a thought, experience, memory, hope, or dream. It can be a response to something you enjoy with your spouse, another person, in a group, by yourself, and even with God. In other words, no two SOULgasms are exactly the same, and they vary in intensity and frequency.

SOULgasm can impact every person. But our primary focus will be married couples. Our desire is to encourage husbands and wives to discover ways to care for their souls—and the soul of their marriage. This includes following godly principles that will open the door to a deeper sense of connection with God and a spouse. Of course, the journey toward increased intimacy involves a lifetime. But our experience is that it begins with the simple step of including God—and then saying *yes!*

Are you ready to say *yes* and take a closer look at what it means to celebrate SOULgasm moments in your life and marriage? We have to warn you, experiencing growth will cost you something. Because when a person says *yes* to the Lord—it includes examination, surrender, trusting God, and taking risks.

Experiencing SOULgasm requires one *yes* at a time. As we begin our authors/reader journey, our challenge for you is a simple one: Throughout this book, keep saying *yes* to God and *yes* to SOULgasm.

PART ONE
SOUL*gasm* Builders

"Love makes your soul crawl out from its hiding place."
Zora Neale Hurston

CHAPTER 1

SOUL WHAT?

SOUL*gasm* was God's idea. God created every human being in His image.[1] And every man and woman have a *spirit*, *soul*, and *body*.[2] The soul is the place where emotions reside. In addition, God gave every person a body to enable them to feel and celebrate emotions and physical sensations. These can include, but are not limited to, joy, sadness, anger, fear, happiness, excitement, and tenderness.

In order to better understand a person's creational design, all you have to do is open the Bible. A main character in the Bible is Jesus Christ. Jesus took on human form and came to earth. He is the quintessential model for what it means to love BIG and live wholeheartedly. The New Testament contains story after story of Jesus expressing a full range of emotions—both positive and negative.

For example, when Jesus experienced loss, the Bible says, "Jesus wept."[3] When He discovered men trying to make money in God's house, He responded with anger, declaring, "My house will be called a house of prayer, but you are making it a 'den of robbers.'"[4] As we've worked with couples, we've seen that anger can be an emotion that Christians are often uncomfortable expressing.

One reason may be that people don't have healthy models for how to express anger in godly ways. Can we ask, *How do you express anger? What do you do when you are violated or discounted?* While Jesus gave us permission to feel all of our feelings, He also modeled how to express them in healthy ways. Regarding anger, the Bible reminds us to, "Be angry and do not sin."[5]

Jesus also experienced fear and anxiety. He responded to fear by pouring out His heart to God, "Father, if it's possible let this cup pass from Me."[6] Again, Jesus gives people permission to express all of their emotions as He modeled how to express them.

With regard to positive emotions, the Bible is full of stories that reveal pleasure, joy, and happiness. For example, God said, "You are My beloved Son, in You I am well-pleased."[7] When Jesus met the Centurion, He said He had never found such great faith in anyone in all of Israel.[8] Imagine how Jesus felt at that moment. We believe He was thrilled and excited. As a matter of fact, we'd suggest that His response could have been described as a SOUL*gasm* moment for Him.

Additional examples include Jesus expressing emotions of gentleness, kindness, and tenderness. One passage described Jesus expressing compassion as He responded to those who were sick: "He saw a large crowd, and felt *compassion* for them and healed their sick."[9] In another instance, Jesus expressed tender emotions relating to children as He rebuked His disciples and said, "Let the children alone, and do not hinder them from coming to Me; for the kingdom of heaven belongs to such as these."[10] Bottom line, God created every human being in His image, and He gave them the ability to express a full range of emotions in both positive and negative ways.

WHO - WHAT - WHEN - WHERE - HOW

Most things can be better understood when *who, what, when, where,* and *how* are addressed.

WHO can experience SOUL*gasm*? Anyone and everyone. This life-giving emotional response is not based on gender or limited to marriage. God designed this human response with *you* in mind. It's for men, women, couples, children, and even something groups of people can experience together. But its audience extends far beyond the human connection—God longs for each person to experience SOUL*gasm* moments with Him as well.

WHAT is a SOUL*gasm*? SOUL*gasm* is unique to humankind because unlike plants and animals, men and women are made in God's image.[11] As we've explained, SOUL*gasm* can be described as an intense surge of joy that pulses through the entire body; it can also be described as a gentle wash of tender emotions that are accompanied by tingling in a person's body—and soul. A SOUL*gasm* can be triggered by an interaction, an act of love or kindness, a thought, memory, hope, or dream. A SOUL*gasm* can be a response to a decision you make to trust God—and take a risk. But regardless of *what* it is a response to, it enriches your soul and heightens your senses. SOUL*gasm* includes a deep sense of satisfaction. SOUL*gasm* moments can be received as gifts from God, a spouse, and others. And because it is an emotional experience, SOUL*gasm* includes transparency and vulnerability.

WHEN can a person experience a SOUL*gasm*? Anytime and anywhere. SOUL*gasm* is something that can catch a person by surprise; and it is also something they can pursue.

WHERE can a person go to find out more about SOUL*gasm*? Well, remember, don't go to *Webster's* because the word is not there! Seriously, we encourage you to always start with God—to **I.O.T.L.** (*Inquire of the Lord*) (Appendix B describes **I.O.T.L.** [*Inquire of the Lord*] in detail.) *Why?* Because SOUL*gasm* was God's idea. He designed every man and woman to experience life-giving emotional moments.

The triune God is all about relationship. Starting in Genesis chapters 1 and 2, "In the beginning ...," before the fall, God invited the first man (before woman was created) into relationship with Him. We imagine God and the man experiencing intimacy and SOUL*gasm* before sin entered the story. After the woman was created out of the man, she entered into relationship with God, and with her husband. The text describes God walking in the garden in the cool of the day[12] where the man and woman lived.

In the beginning, God commanded the man and woman to "become one,"[13] and He described them as being "naked and [they] were not ashamed."[14] It's interesting to note that before God created the woman, He described everything He created as "good." But after God created the woman, He described everything He created as "very good."[15] Just imagine what life was like in Paradise! Surely their souls were bursting with joy. SOUL*gasms* were not limited by time, SOUL*gasm* was a lifestyle. Paradise continued until sin disrupted God's original design for oneness, equality, and mutuality.

HOW does a person measure SOUL*gasm*? Imagine for a moment there was a way to measure the effects of this phenomenon on a continuum. Let's say an intense emotional response of positivity would be rated a 9-10, while a gentle wash of positivity might be rated a 3-4. Regardless of how it rates on the continuum, every SOUL*gasm* experience is unique because every person is unique. Even the physical sensations that accompany SOUL*gasm* moments vary.

The good news is that God offers every person, and couple, opportunities to discover new ways to care for their soul and the soul of their marriage. His principles invite them to consider how to *build* on SOUL*gasm* experiences as well as resist behaviors that *block* them.

EXTRAORDINARY AND ORDINARY MOMENTS

When a person experiences an *extraordinary* mountaintop moment, it creates a SOUL*gasm* experience. When this occurs, the physical body responds by releasing the famous quartet of feel-good chemicals— dopamine, serotonin, oxytocin, and endorphins. And together they create sensations that put a simple adrenaline rush to shame. In addition to *extraordinary* moments, God created people to experience deep SOUL*gasm* sensations of joy and connection in life's everyday *ordinary* moments. Don't get us wrong, everyone loves mountaintop moments. But you don't need to depend on occasional *extraordinary* moments to awaken your soul or heighten your senses. SOUL*gasm* moments are available through *ordinary* experiences in life and marriage. And when viewed from the correct perspective, *ordinary* moments can become *extraordinary* moments. We think the following quote by Frederick Buechner captures celebrating the *extraordinary* in the *ordinary* things in life:

> As you learn to listen to your life and what God is doing in it, you will uncover the plot of your life's story and the sacred opportunity to connect with the divine in each moment.
>
> Pay attention, says Buechner. Listen to the call of a bird or the rush of the wind, of the people who flow in and out of your life. The ordinary points you to the extraordinary God who created and loves all of creation,

including you. Pay attention to these things as if your life depends on it. Because, of course, it does.[16]

We often remind our clients of the Enemy's strategy to steal *extraordinary* and *ordinary* moments. He does this by subtly persuading a person to live in the past with regret or to live in the future with anxiety. A key to enjoying *extraordinary* and *ordinary* moments is to choose to live in the present—the *now*. As simple as that sounds, living in the moment is a discipline that a person can choose to practice for a lifetime.

As we've talked with couples, we've seen that as they look back over their lives, they often share how it was the small (*ordinary*) things that were really the big (*extraordinary*) things. Remember, *extraordinary* and *ordinary* moments that lead to experiencing SOUL*gasm* can be experienced in a variety of ways. Following are a few examples:

+ Two friends reach the top of a 14,000-foot summit. Their shared victory is accompanied by a gentle wash of joy pulsing through their bodies. In an instant and without warning, a hiking challenge becomes a deep emotionally satisfying experience. An *extraordinary* moment—both individually and together—leads to SOUL*gasm!*

+ It's the end of a long but very ordinary day; a wife sits with her husband on their backyard swing. Together, side by side, they watch their children playing in the yard. Without a word, they are caught off guard by the sounds of their children's voices, the smell of charcoal on the grill, and the feeling of damp grass under their bare feet. Their senses are heightened as a warm wash of gratitude and contentment fills their souls. In an instant and without warning, an *ordinary* moment becomes an *extraordinary* moment—they experience SOUL*gasm!*

+ T.G.I.F. (*Thank God it's Friday*) After a full and tiring week for both of them, a husband decides to surprise his wife. Realizing that she needs a break, he orders pizza for the kids, and knowing how much she loves to drive, he suggests she take their new car for a drive while he gets the kids fed and to bed. Without any real plans or a specific destination in mind, she kisses them all goodbye and gets in the car. First stop is for coffee, she fills her travel mug. Sitting in the parking lot, she flips through the Sirius satellite radio stations, planning her next move. Pulling out onto the open road, she rolls down the windows and turns up the volume. She takes in a few deep breaths and exhales the tension from the week. She can't remember the last time she was alone without someone tugging on her body—and soul. Completely exhausted by the stress of raising a young family, tears fill her eyes and spill down her cheeks. She lets the music wash over her soul as she sips her hot coffee and enjoys the simple pleasure of solitude—she drives. During this time, she becomes keenly aware that despite life's challenges she is loved by God, by her sweet husband, and her precious littles. A rare but very *ordinary* moment becomes an *extraordinary* gift— and a leisurely drive turns into a SOUL*gasm* experience!

+ Consider the excitement that rises in a die-hard Chicago Cubs baseball fan as she sits in the bleachers at Wrigley Field; taking in all the sights, smells, and sounds of that amazing ballpark. Hearing the roar of the crowd as a bat cracks a homerun onto Waveland Avenue. In an instant and without warning, an *ordinary* moment becomes an *extraordinary* moment—and she experiences SOUL*gasm!*

+ Consider the growing tension between two people as they choose to work through some conflict that has caused them both pain. Each takes ownership and responsibility to process through hurts in their relationship. Before they experience breakthrough, difficult words are exchanged, accusations are processed, grace is extended, and for-giveness is offered. In an instant and without warning, a painfully honest conversation becomes an *extraordinary* moment—and they experience SOUL*gasm!*

+ Imagine the intense emotional pleasure experienced by a grandparent. Whether they are actually engaging with their grandchildren or merely thinking about them, they are filled with a deep sense of satisfaction. In an instant, without warning, a rush of joy floods his or her soul. An *ordinary* moment becomes *extraordinary*—and they experience SOUL*gasm!*

Experiences like the ones listed above can become opportunities for a person to soak in. They can become priceless gifts as *ordinary* moments become *extraordinary*—and they open the door to experience SOUL*gasm.*

SOUL*GASM* IN MARRIAGE

We love being married. But even after forty-plus years, those words have come with a price. Experiencing SOUL*gasm* in marriage is not about following a list of steps or pretending there are easy solutions to life's problems. In fact, many of the stories we share do not end with a pink bow. *Why?* Because marriage was never designed to be a fairy-tale fantasy about a never-ending honeymoon. Marriage is an invitation to journey with God and surrender control to Him. It's an opportunity to trust Him to provide you with security and significance in ways that no one else can.

First Corinthians 7:28 (NIV) says, "Those who marry will face many troubles in this life." We've been married for decades. We have four children, three of them are married, and five grandchildren. We've experienced plenty of good times, and we've also lived through troubling times. Personally, we refuse to allow troubles to define our marriage. Our experience has taught us that the key to dealing with marriage troubles is how a husband/wife responds to troubles. Do they view them as *obstacles* or *opportunities*?

Experiencing troubles is a normal part of marriage. Going through difficult times invites a couple to review covenant, and to better understand grace and forgiveness. As we reflect on our marriage, when we say *we love being married*, the main reason we make that statement is intimately related to God. *Why?* Because God created marriage. And one of our ongoing marriage desires is to advance in intimacy—in knowing and being fully known—by God, and with each other.

INTIMACY—TO KNOW AND BE FULLY KNOWN

What comes to mind when you hear the word *intimacy*? While there are many ways to describe the word, we define intimacy as *to know and be fully known*.[17] You may have heard the word broken down into syllables that read: *into-me-you-see*. Remember, SOUL*gasm* was God's idea. He designed every human being with a *spirit*, *soul*, and *body*.[18] In marriage, SOUL*gasm* moments are gifts that increase the spiritual, emotional, and physical connection between a husband and wife.

SOUL*gasm* becomes a pathway to grow in intimacy—knowing and being fully known. This involves experiences that bond a husband and wife to each other within the lifelong covenant of marriage.

So far, we have presented SOUL*gasm* as emotional pleasure rather than sexual pleasure. However, as a married couple advances in emotional intimacy, it has a positive impact on their sexual intimacy. In marriage, men and women are invited to experience intimate moments that deepen a couples understanding of what it means to "become one."[19] And these moments include emotional and sexual pleasure. We will talk more about SOUL*gasm* sex in chapter 7.

MATURITY IS A CHOICE

Whenever we observe couples who are emotionally connected, we know they have qualities we can learn from. When we look a little deeper, we discover they share a level of maturity that supports their relationship rather than works against it. One of the qualities that stands out with couples who are emotionally connected is their willingness to take ownership and responsibility for their part in marriage. It seems they are not afraid to say, *"I am sorry. I was wrong. Will you forgive me?"* Being able to take ownership for the ways they have offended their spouse frees them up to advance in intimacy.

If you were able to take a close-up look at how emotionally connected couples practically walk out their lives, you would observe a number of qualities. For example, you will see mature husbands and wives who are willing to take ownership and responsibility for their lives. They are willing to put away childish things in exchange for deeper intimacy. Emotionally connected couples are teachable and quick to admit they have things to learn. Husbands and wives who advance in personal maturity advance in intimacy with God, their spouse, and others.

Throughout this book we are not offering simple formulas with guaranteed outcomes. What we are offering are godly principals that can strengthen a couple's foundation and enable them to live in greater harmony and experience more frequent SOUL*gasm* moments.

One of the most famous passages in the Bible is referred to as "the love chapter"—1 Corinthians 13. We'd like to highlight a few passages. First, verse 9 says, "We know in part." The truth is every person has things they can learn. In marriage, couples who understand that they do not know everything—*who know in part*—are husbands and wives who are humble—and teachable. Humble and teachable people are willing to take ownership and responsibility in their lives, including marriage. First Corinthians chapter 13, verse 11 (NIV), says, "When I was a child, I talked like a child, I thought like a child, I reasoned like a child. When I became a man, I put the ways of childhood behind me."

If you were sitting in our counseling office, it wouldn't take long before you realized we have different styles of counseling. After a career spanning more than twenty years on the fire department, I (Tim) tend to be much more direct than Anne. On a number of occasions, after listening intentionally, I will look a person in the eyes and lovingly say, "I believe your problem is not as complicated as you may think. I wonder what it would look like if, instead of investing a lot of time, energy, and resources in more counseling appointments, you simply spent time focusing on First Corinthians 13:11, and made intentional choices to *grow up*?"

Another important marriage lesson we've learned (in addition to "every marriage experiences troubles"[20] and people need to grow up) is that marriage takes a lot of hard work. But in our experience, doing the hard work of marriage is the best investment we've ever made. Choosing to invest your time, energy, resources, and passion into your marriage will bring you a rich return on your investment.

LIVING WITH A HEART THAT IS FULLY ALIVE

Husbands and wives who experience regular SOUL*gasm* moments come in all races, ages, and denominations. They are people who desire to grow in understanding their identity, which includes learning what it means to be comfortable in their own skin. We would describe them as people who place a high value on living in the present and are able to joyfully celebrate the *extraordinary* and *ordinary* moments in life—and marriage. We have observed them as people who are good listeners and who understand the importance of direct eye contact. They are quick to forgive and presuppose the best in others. And they are intentional as they look for ways to model love and kindness to each other.

Couples who understand the bonding power of SOUL*gasm* moments are able to enjoy non-sexual (as well as sexual) touch as expressions of love. And they have learned how to laugh together. Surely you have observed couples like that. They seem to genuinely enjoy each other's company. If you listen closely, you will overhear vulnerable exchanges that reflect kindness and respect, such as *Please … Thank you … Help me understand … It concerns me when … How can I be with you? … I believe in you … I want the best for you.* These loving exchanges are a symbol of the rich deposits an emotionally connected couple regularly invests into their intimacy account.

We said earlier that life is hard. This is another reason why it's so important to look for opportunities to celebrate life. Whether you are celebrating yourself, your spouse, or the wonder found in *ordinary* and *extraordinary* moments—these can all reflect a sense of gratitude. This leads to living with a fully alive heart and celebrating your spouse. And this becomes the pathway to living in the Larger Story with *God* as the main character; instead of living in the smaller story where *self* is the main character. We will look deeper at this concept in upcoming chapters. For these couples, marriage is "not about 'ME,' but about 'WE.'"[21] In the next chapter, we will unpack how a husband and wife's family of origin can positively and negatively impact a couple's intimacy and ability to experience SOUL*gasm*.

CHAPTER 2

UNDERSTANDING YOUR FAMILY OF ORIGIN

When we got married, we had no idea how much the families we came from—our families of origin—would influence our relationship, intimacy, and decision-making process. As newlyweds, we quickly realized that our marriage included more than just two of us. It included our families of origin.

Whenever we talk to premarital couples, we remind them that when they marry their spouse, they are also marrying into their spouse's family. Of course, the covenant they are making is with God and each other—but the *influence* each family has on a couple's relationship and marriage will continue to provide both *opportunities* and *obstacles* for growth. That means that the decisions a husband and wife make as a result of their family's influence will contribute to *building*—or *blocking*—SOUL*gasm* moments.

Part of the story God is telling through each of our lives involves our family. That includes everyone's histories, experiences, propensities, behaviors, and beliefs, just to name a few. This is one reason why it's so important for couples to recognize the influence their family of origin has on their life, and in their marriage.

When our children began seriously dating, we encouraged them to get to know the family of the person they were dating. We would challenge them to pay close attention to the following: how the family members related to each other; how they communicated; how they resolved conflict; and how they handled finances and stress. We told them to consider: How do the parents relate to one another, and what kind of relationship do the children have with their parents? Are the family members forgiving people, quick to admit when they are wrong? Do they apologize to one another? Are there negative patterns or destructive cycles that they seem to be unwilling to deal with in healthy ways?

Life is lived in a story

anne

I remember when our daughter Colleen started getting serious about a young man she'd been dating. His name was Johnny Stickl. At that time, he was a student at Denver Seminary where he was completing his master's in Christian leadership. He was also interning at our church and attending leadership classes at the World Prayer Center where Tim and I worked. In fact, Tim set them up on their first date (but that's another story!). So while Johnny was living in Colorado, he got a chance to know our family pretty well.

However, Johnny's family lived in Grand Island, New York, so Colleen hadn't yet had the opportunity to meet them or observe Johnny in his home environment. As we started to sense their relationship could be leading to marriage, Tim and I encouraged Colleen to spend time getting acquainted with Johnny's family.

The two of them made plans and flew to New York to visit with his family. One night after dinner, Colleen called to let me know how things were going. She began the conversation by saying, "Mom, their family is *sooo* different from ours."

Her observation concerned me, so I asked, "What do you mean?"

"Well, one example is meal times. When we had dinner tonight, only *one person* talked at a time. Can you imagine that?" She laughed, adding, "During meal times in our home, it's hard to complete a sentence without being interrupted. We have to talk over each other if we want to be heard. But Johnny's family actually listened to every word I said—*it was amazing!*"

I asked, "What did you talk about?"

"I started telling them about school and specific areas of study I'm interested in. As I talked, everyone was quiet and listened to me—without interrupting. When I was finished, there was a long pause. Johnny's mom said something like, 'Colleen, that's so interesting. Let me ask you a question about that.' Mom, it was unbelievable—she actually listened to every word I said."

I interrupted, "Honey, that's how *normal people* relate to one another!"

EVERY FAMILY HAS A "DANCE"

Every family is unique. They have their own style of relating, and their own way of doing things. Some of the things that make a person's family unique include their beliefs and traditions. Families also have certain incli-nations, tendencies, and propensities. Whenever we counsel couples, or teach at REAL LIFE marriage gatherings, we often refer to some of these distinct family traits, patterns, and behaviors as the *family dance*.

It's been said that some of the most powerful lessons a person learns are caught rather than taught. For example, children learn how to navigate their world by observing their family—how they communicate, how they listen, how they forgive, how they relate to God and each other, how they process problems, make decisions, and deal with life. Children grow up with a perception of who they are based on what they've observed. All of these observations influence the way they negotiate their world, even as adults.

Their belief system, perceptions, behaviors, and general approach to life are a part of the *dance* they learned from observing their family of origin. And especially in marriage, a husband and wife's family of origin impacts their intimacy and ability to understand, experience, and celebrate SOUL*gasm*.

Stop and think about it. Most people can predict how their family will respond to any given situation.

For example, a person knows what their family considers funny and what is not funny. They know what is acceptable and what is off limits. How do they know this? Because (figuratively speaking) they've watched their family dance the same steps over and over again. Sometimes the mes-sage was clearly verbalized, but more often it was conveyed in nonverbal ways.

The dance pattern can vary dramatically from family to family. For example, in some families, divorce is not an option. In other families, divorce is considered an acceptable alternative. In premarital counseling sessions, we have actually heard engaged couples say, "If this marriage doesn't work out, we can always get divorced—just like our parents did."

When a new spouse is overly focused on their own family dance, it can hinder the process of learning a new dance together as a couple. And this can threaten potential SOUL*gasm* moments. For example, imagine a husband and wife on the dance floor, one doing the tango, while the other is doing the salsa, and both trying to move in unison. Inevitably, they will collide or drift apart, rather than enjoy the intimacy and beauty of a shared rhythm.

When we got married, it didn't take long before we discovered that Anne's family dance followed a very different beat from Tim's family dance. When we tried to dance together, we would often end up stepping on each other's toes. We couldn't believe the other person didn't dance the way we did, the way our family did—the "right way." We were quick to accuse each other of coming from a long line of dysfunctional dancers! Accusations turned into offenses, and this led to power struggles. Before long, each of us was trying to control the dance, and we would argue about who's family dance was going to lead. You can only imagine how these choices *blocked* the SOUL*gasm* moments we longed for.

Like every married couple, we came from two different families with their own unique ways of doing things. We wondered: *Which family dance is the right dance?* More importantly, we longed to learn a new dance—*together* as a couple.

Life is lived in a story

anne

I can still recall a dream I had years ago when we lived in Michigan. It helped me understand the family dances that Tim and I brought into our marriage. In my dream a man and a woman, both dressed in white, stood on separate sides of a large stage, unaware of each other's presence. Each of them stared intently at the bright spotlight above them. Somehow, I knew each of their spotlights represented the Lord. He was their guiding light, the ONE who was leading them.

As the orchestra music began to play, the man and woman were learning how to move around the stage in unison with their spotlight. The Lord was teaching each of them the dance of unconditional love, the dance of forgiveness, the dance of communication, and the dance of surrender. If they took a wrong turn, the Lord gently redirected them. Their individual sense of joy and unity with God was defined by SOUL*gasm* moments.

Suddenly, the music stopped, and the man and woman became aware of each other. With a sense of mutual fascination, they followed their spotlight across the room toward each other. The man and woman stood face to face. As they embraced, their individual spotlights merged into one single bright light above them. And the music started up again. This time, a new song began to play. The man clasped the woman's hand in his. With his other arm encircling her waist, they began to dance together. As they danced, there were no awkward steps. Instead, they moved around the dance floor in unity as one. They knew how to dance with each other because they had learned how to dance with the Lord. Trusting Him *first* allowed them to trust Him *together*. He was the ONE who prepared them to dance in unity and mutuality.

When I woke up, I knew that God was inviting me to dance with Him. He longs to lead every person in the dance of intimacy—first with Him and then with others. In marriage, God teaches a husband and wife the dance of mutual equality (both intrinsically and functionally). He leads them in the dance of unconditional love, mutual authority, and reciprocal servanthood. As God continues to teach a husband and wife to advance in intimacy, He also invites them to experience a deep sense of joy and SOUL*gasm* moments.

Dancing in unity with your spouse often requires *unlearning* some of the dance steps you learned from your family of origin. But before you can learn a new dance together, it's important to understand what dance you learned as a child and are currently doing now. That requires a willingness to take an honest and objective look at your respective families of origin. Depending on your family history, that process often requires the help of a godly counselor or objective third party. Failing to process negative family patterns often *blocks* couples from growing in intimacy and experiencing SOUL*gasm* moments.

DESIGNING A LEGACY

Every person has received a legacy from God—their inheritance or birthright. "A legacy is something that is handed down or remains from a previous generation or time."[1] And every person will leave a legacy to those who come after them. Legacies include many components: spiritual, emotional, relational, physical, sexual, and health-related components, along with associated beliefs, behaviors, and propensities that are passed down from generation to generation. Remember, all of these components can include both positive and negative aspects.

What behaviors, beliefs, and propensities have been handed down in your family of origin? A godly spiritual legacy is a gift from your ancestors and can lead to experiencing SOUL*gasm* moments. But an ungodly spiritual legacy can *block* couples from experiencing SOUL*gasm*.

In counseling sessions over the years, we've seen many benefits for couples willing to explore the patterns and propensities from their families of origin. These couples are better equipped to move toward increased intimacy and walk in unity. Knowing and understanding histories and families of origin, including where a person came from and what they received from their ancestors, enables a couple to identify positive godly components from their family line, and *build* on them. It also enables a couple to identify negative, ungodly components that they do not want to continue in their marriage. Can we ask, *What positive and negative propensities, values, and behaviors were present in your, and your spouse's, families of origin?*

THE APPLE DOESN'T FALL FAR FROM THE TREE

There is an old adage that says, *The apple doesn't fall far from the tree.* A tree produces both good and bad fruit. Likewise, a *family tree* also produces good and bad fruit. Not only do we inherit physical features, mannerisms, and speech patterns—we also inherit the consequences of positive and negative propensities, behaviors, and beliefs.

Growing up, we were never taught anything related to how our ancestors' choices and behaviors could be impacting us. These family influences can be called generational propensities. The truth is that God is a generational God—the God of Abraham, Isaac, and Jacob. And the Bible describes how our ancestors' choices can affect future generations. Exodus 20:5 (NIV) says, "I, the LORD your God, am a jealous God, punishing the children for the sin of the parents to the third and fourth generation of those who hate me." This verse is a reminder that a person's generational line impacts their life.

Negative and positive generational propensities are different for every family. They can include negative behaviors such as pride, unrighteous judging, unforgiveness, addictive behaviors, violence, and rebellion. Understanding the impact negative propensities and behaviors have on a person's life, and marriage, hopefully increases their desire for freedom.

But there is another side of Exodus 20 that often gets overlooked. Generational propensities also include positive behaviors and blessings. Verse 6 reminds us that God, "shows lovingkindness to a thousand generations of those who love me and keep my commandments." So, imagine the generational impact on a family line when a person makes godly decisions to live with integrity, be honest and trustworthy, have financial integrity, and maintain a strong work ethic. This Bible promise encourages and challenges a person to trust God and live by godly principles.

When a couple gets married, blending two families together is not as easy as it may sound. Especially when it comes to cherished family traditions that have been practiced for generations. It's part of a person's human nature to desire to stick with what is familiar—even if it's unhealthy. Frankly, it's more difficult to create a "new normal" together with your spouse. That's why relationship with God is so important. As a husband and wife choose to let go of the family dance that is familiar to them, as they trust God and risk walking through unchartered territory, they quickly realize that God is the key to experiencing breakthrough and victory from repeating negative generational propensities and cycles.

God created every man and woman as a volitional human being who has been given the freedom and ability to make choices. Regardless of family-of-origin experiences, or mistakes that have been made in the past, no one has to live as a victim of life's circumstances. Our good Father will never force a person to obey. Instead He gives them the freedom to choose Him, to choose right or wrong, obedience or disobedience, and a path that leads to death or life. In marriage, the key to dancing together in unity is to follow God's creational design, to make choices that *build* on life-giving behaviors and beliefs, as well as identifying and eliminating negative ones.

It's encouraging for us to walk with couples as they prayerfully process and agree on propensities they want to keep and *build* on; as well as seeing them agree on ones they want to discontinue. Positive motivations for working through these issues include experiencing unity in marriage, and passing on life-giving family behaviors and beliefs to children, grandchildren—and to future generations. Often after working through family-of-origin issues, a husband or wife will share with us, "I truly believed *my way* was the *best way*. But as I included God and processed *my way* with my spouse, we are now together experiencing amazing *new ways*."

Life is lived in a story

anne

We counseled a couple who were planning to get married. We'll call them "Scott and Sandy." As we reviewed their histories, we took note of their families of origin, and we began to identify some of the negative and positives aspects in the legacies from their family lines. They both came from divorced homes. Each of them had family members on both sides who struggled with alcoholism and other addictive behaviors.

At their first few appointments, Scott and Sandy were unaware of how much their families of origin propensities, behaviors, and beliefs had influenced them. But as we continued to meet, they began to see some destructive patterns they were experiencing that were similar to what they had seen while growing up. For example, Sandy had strained relationships with her father and her stepfather, and those complicated feelings toward the men in her family contributed to her experiencing a strained relationship with her future husband. Scott was prone to controlling behavior and outbursts of anger, just like his father. Scott and Sandy didn't understand how these negative patterns were affecting them individually—and as a couple.

Both of them genuinely wanted a strong marriage. They wanted more for themselves and their future family than what they'd experienced while growing up. We encouraged them with the Bible passage that says, "Anyone who belongs to Christ has become a new person. The old life is gone; a new life has begun!"[2] Scott and Sandy were determined to pass on a godly legacy to their children, and to future generations. And they knew the journey had to begin with them. Recognizing the value of community, they joined a small group, and agreed to a season of counseling. They were both teachable and willing to look at their past to see how it affected their present, and how it could impact their future.

They both began to identify negative patterns in the ways they tried to resolve conflict. The only models they'd had for conflict resolution had come from their families of origin. The result was a destructive and controlling dance that *blocked* intimacy. Thankfully, they were both open to learning a *new dance* with God—and with each other. One of the first decisions they made was to never use divorce as a threat during an argument. Instead, they adopted new healthy ways to manage their emotions. This was a strong start toward advancing in intimacy with God and each other. Each small step became an invitation for Scott and Sandy to experience both small and amazing SOUL*gasm* moments.

Scott and Sandy understood the journey toward increased intimacy with God and each other would become a lifelong journey. They passionately committed to getting rid of negative behaviors and replacing them with positive life-giving ones. They understood that this would bless them, their future children, and future generations.

Regardless of your family of origin, the best first step in every journey involves saying *yes* to the Lord. Scott and Sandy said *yes,* they both trusted God—and took risks. They were willing to take a closer look at what it meant to *build* and *block* SOUL*gasm* moments in their lives and marriage. But remember, saying *yes* to the Lord will always cost you something. And that price usually includes being willing to examine your heart and life, and surrender to God. While there are no quick fixes, easy applications, or simple solutions—one *yes* to God at a time will yield increased intimacy and SOUL*gasm* experiences, resulting in a generational harvest of godly fruit.

Throughout decades of counseling couples and individuals, we've seen that family-of-origin issues inevitably surface. We challenge couples—we challenge *you*—to view troubles not as *obstacles*, but as *opportunities* to advance in intimacy with God and with your spouse. Give each other lots of grace because negotiating family-of-origin differences is a lifelong process. We challenge you to put *your* way, and *your* family dance aside, and choose to let God introduce new dance steps. Our experience is that when this happens, husbands and wives find themselves moving toward a rhythm of unity that blends the best of both families.

All that is to say, the best personal, and marital, advice we can offer is to begin everything with **I.O.T.L.** (We will explore **I.O.T.L.** in upcoming chapters and in Appendix B.) Invite God into your process and ask for wisdom. The Bible makes this amazing promise: "If any of you lacks of wisdom, let him ask of God, who gives to all generously and without reproach."[3] Learning to recognize God's voice, responding with a "yes" attitude, and being willing to give up *your* way, becomes the pathway to advance in intimacy and experience SOUL*gasm*.

CHAPTER 3

CELEBRATING YOUR SPOUSE'S UNIQUENESS

Life is lived in a story

anne

It's fun to work with premarital couples because they are in an "intoxi-cated-love" state. Tim and I enjoyed that intoxicated state early in our relationship. When we were dating, I could make up an endless list of all the things that attracted me to Tim. I loved everything about him. I loved that he was decisive; I was attracted to his strength and strong leader-ship. He was direct, focused, and confident. The ways he processed life distinguished him from every other person I had ever met.

However, marriage and real life have a way of moving a couple out of the intoxicated phase of their relationship and, figuratively speaking, sober-ing them up. After being married a year or so, I remember looking at Tim and saying, "I don't understand the ways you process life. Are you always so strong, so sure of yourself, and so decisive?" The differences that I once thought were so wonderful suddenly bothered me. I often thought to myself, *What is his problem? Why can't he be more like ME? Why can't he think more like ME? Why can't he respond to life more like I do?* Apparently, I thought I was the prototype for perfection. The answer to every problem seemed to focus on Tim changing and becoming more like ME.

+ + +

We were teaching at a REAL LIFE Marriage Advance and mentioned how newlyweds are "intoxicated" with love. After the session, a couple approached us and asked, "Once we get married, how can we stay intoxicated?" We replied, "That's a good question," and we shared some of our thoughts. But after that gathering, we wrote down the following ten ways for newlyweds to stay "intoxicated." Of course, the following can also help married couples to reclaim "intoxicating" times.

1. **Every marriage experiences troubles.**[1] The "intoxicated" season of dating and being a newlywed is a time of intense bonding, and it includes the early stages of intimacy. However, the Bible reminds every couple—newlyweds to seasoned couples—that "those who marry will face many troubles." This verse reminds couples that *troubles* are normal and have potential to lead a couple into deeper intimacy. So, when marital *troubles* threaten to sober a couple up, we encourage them to be open to learning new ways to successfully process through their *troubles*. This journey requires maturity, but it can become a huge intimacy *builder* that leads to deeper levels of "intoxication." So, don't be afraid of *troubles*—they are normal. Let them be your pathway to deeper intimacy.

2. **We encourage couples to grow in understanding God's creational marriage design.** Consider this: People will invest time, energy, and resources in learning about parenting, developing a career, or enjoying a hobby. But often after getting married, couples inordinately focus on jobs-kids-finances. And this can inhibit the ongoing exploration of the incredible miracle and mystery of how "two become one,"[2] and celebrating being "naked without shame."[3]

3. **We encourage couples to take seriously the command to "leave and cleave."[4]** Identify the relationships, activities, responsibilities, behaviors, and so on, that you were involved with as a single person. When you get married, determine if you need to *leave* any of these so you can fully *cleave* to your spouse. Relating to family of origin, focus on keeping all the good things from each family, and leave behind the not-so-good things.

4. **We encourage couples to intentionally invest in knowing and understanding themselves.[5]** Continue taking steps to better understand what it truly means to be made in the image of a good God.[6] This allows a person to step into their true identity as God's *beloved* son or daughter. And it enables them to better Reflect and Reveal God's love, grace, plurality, and goodness to a spouse (and others).

5. **We encourage couples to invest in healing and Christ-centered counseling.** Scripture says, "Where

there is no guidance the people fall, But in abundance of counselors there is victory."[7] Don't wait until you are in crisis to ask for help. Invest in regular marriage tune-ups and attend workshops and seminars that will help you identify and address areas that need to be worked on. This will enable you to become a more life-giving spouse—and couple.

6. **We encourage couples to practice a lifestyle that is grounded in grace and forgiveness.** A simple two-word definition of marriage is "inexhaustible forgiveness." Couples who default to forgiveness, and who live out marriages where "It's not all about me," tend to live more blessed and joy-filled lives. Remember, forgiveness begins with a decision. It includes asking a spouse for forgiveness for things you did (commission); as well as asking a spouse for forgiveness for things you failed to do (omission). Of course, receiving forgiveness from God, and forgiving yourself, are important keys to understanding and living out forgiveness.

7. **We encourage couples to develop the habit of making decisions in unity with God and your spouse by implementing the Traffic Light Principle** (see Appendix C). Intentionally include Him as you **I.O.T.L.** Then, wait until you and your spouse have "green lights" from God and with each other before pulling the trigger on decisions. In marriage, unity should always trump disunity.

8. **We encourage couples to have regular D.O.F. days (Days of Fun).** Plan times (weekly, bi-weekly, at least monthly) with the goal of totally focusing on enjoying each other. This can include rest, relaxation, romance, and refreshment—without guilt or excuses. Share your dreams and desires, and together pray for your life and marriage.

9. **We encourage couples to celebrate SPIRIT + SOUL + BODY oneness.** SPIRIT oneness is an invitation to grow in your relationship with your good Father. It includes learning what it means to be intimately connected to God, and this becomes a model for what it means to be intimately connected with your spouse. SOUL oneness is an invitation to grow in intimacy, in knowing and being fully known, in treasuring *ordinary* and *extraordinary* moments, and in experiencing SOUL*gasm*. BODY oneness is an invitation to grow in understanding each other's bodies and celebrating God's one-of-a-kind gift of being "naked and not ashamed."[8] A healthy sex life should include experiencing orgasms (remember, orgasms were God's idea). Sexual intimacy includes a deep bond that strengthens a couple's relationship. Taking steps to nurture your SPIRIT, SOUL, and BODY is an important part of staying intoxicated in marriage.

10. **We encourage couples with this slogan:** *Fail to plan; plan to fail.* Decide now to make strategic investments of time, energy, passion, and resources into

your marriage. Learn to say *YES* to the God things, and *NO* to many other things. In doing so, you will be making your marriage a top life priority.

On a personal note, in ways a young couple may find difficult to understand, marriage has taught us more about God and ourselves than any other relationship in our lives. Figuratively speaking, our intoxication is no longer the kind of high a person might get from a cheap bottle of *Two-Buck-Chuck*. Instead, our intoxication is the kind of high a person gets from enjoying an expensive bottle of French champagne, such as *Dom Perignon*. But a good wine, like a good marriage, takes time and must be nurtured.

SPIRITUAL GIFTS

One of the blessings of receiving much of our early spiritual formation training at Willow Creek Community Church was learning about the importance of knowing your spiritual gifts. As we've grown in understanding our individual and each other's spiritual gifts, this has continued to positively impact our marriage in countless ways. God gives spiritual gifts to every follower of Christ. They play an important role in how a person functions in life, marriage, and in the church. As Christ-followers, it is our responsibility to nurture, grow, and steward the spiritual gifts God has given us. If you don't know your spiritual gifts, a number of tools are available to help you identify and better understand them.[9]

The Bible uses the human body to illustrate the spiritual gifts principle. Each part of a person's physical body was created by God with a specific purpose and function. In a healthy body, the individual parts work together effectively. It is the same with spiritual gifts. Every person is given gifts that have a specific purpose and function in building up the church and advancing the kingdom of God. Dr. C. Peter Wagner highlights the importance of identifying spiritual gifts: "I do not think I am amiss in stating that one of the primary spiritual exercises for any Christian person is to discover, develop, and use his or her spiritual gift."[10] God gives spiritual gifts to help the church function in healthy ways, but spiritual gifts are also important in marriage. A life-giving marriage includes a husband and wife who have identified their spiritual gifts and celebrate them in oneness and community—without comparison or competition. For example, we know a couple who love to take on service projects together—such as adopting a family for Christmas or taking food to a family at Thanksgiving. They describe how these moments bring them closer together emotionally and spiritually. For them, serving together helps them experience SOUL*gasm*.

Life is lived in a story

anne

When the two of us decided to leave our jobs and step into REAL LIFE Ministries full time, God used our spiritual gifts to help us reach unity in the decision-making process. This was a busy season for us. Our daughter Amy was pregnant and awaiting the arrival of our first grandchild. Our daughter Colleen got engaged and was planning an out-of-state wedding in Chicago. Our son, Tim, was completing his master's degree in social work. Our youngest daughter Cate was a full-time college student. Obviously, we had a lot going on in our family.

Our spiritual gifts became invaluable as we co-led together. Tim's gift of leadership provided the direction we needed, while his gifts of encouragement, faith, and prayer kept us steady and provided protection during difficult times. While Tim is more of a big-picture thinker who provides direction and vision, God used my gifts of wisdom and discernment to evaluate specific situations and see things that might be overlooked.

As Tim and I continue to work together in unity, our spiritual gifts complement each other and enable us to Reflect and Reveal the plurality and diversity within the Trinity. Of course, no human being, or couple, can fully reflect the triune God because God is God—and we are not. However, gifts provide a person, and couple, with strength and protection. When a husband or wife uses the gifts God has given them, and encourages their spouse to do the same, *together* they will advance in oneness, intimacy— and experience SOUL*gasm*.

TEMPERAMENTS AND STYLES OF RELATING

It is amazing to see lights go on for couples as they gain a greater understanding of how God has wired them. Truly understanding each other's temperaments increases a couple's intimacy and opens the door for them to experience SOUL*gasm*. Remember, every person is unique, and is born with different personalities and temperaments. These include a person's nature, outlook on life, and disposition. If you don't already know your temperament, a number of tools are available to help you identify and understand how your approach to life may be different from your spouse's. For example, the DISC model for evaluating behavioral styles and preferences describes the four basic temperament types: Choleric (D-type), Sanguine (I-type), Phlegmatic (S-type) and Melancholy (C-type).[11] Another tool is the Taylor-Johnson Temperament Analysis (TJTA), which measures nine personality traits and their opposites.[12]

Life is lived in a story

tim

I have grown to more fully appreciate our marriage by understanding how our temperaments affect our interactions with each other and with other people. We've learned that Anne is melancholy. She is quieter, content to listen, analytical, and much more introspective than I am. She is an observer of life. Spending time alone recharges her. Socially, she prefers a few deep relationships rather than large groups of people. By contrast, I am sanguine and choleric. I love people—lots of people. Relating with others energizes me. At the same time, I have a serious side. I'm pragmatic in my leadership style as I focus on goals and action plans, facts and results.

Over the years, God has used Anne to model different aspects of His nature to me. Her lifestyle has taught me how to be still and enjoy solitude. Being still before God allows me to see Him, myself, and others in new ways. And slowing my pace of life down encourages me to better recognize the *ordinary* and *extraordinary* moments in my life and marriage. At the same time, Anne's world has expanded by being with me. She tells me that my positive outlook on life, love for people, and outgoing nature has encouraged her to embrace each moment and be more adventuresome and spontaneous. Our different temperaments and styles of relating allow us to Reflect and Reveal a clearer image of God than either one of us could do alone. It also helps us to advance in intimacy, and experience SOUL*gasm*.

SPEAKING YOUR SPOUSE'S LOVE LANGUAGE

Closely connected to the topic of individual temperaments and relational styles is the idea that everyone has their own love language. In other words, certain things make them feel more loved than others. Dr. Gary Chapman's book *The Five Love Languages* describes specific ways we give and receive love: words of affirmation, quality time, gifts, acts of service, and physical touch.[13] Readers are challenged to identify their primary love languages—the ways they feel most loved—and to learn how to speak the love language of the people they value.

Life is lived in a story

tim

Years ago, we counseled a newly married couple that we will refer to as "Roger and Sally." When we first began to see them, they had never heard about love languages. Roger grew up in a stoic family that was uncomfortable with displays of affection. In fact, Roger could not remember his parents ever holding hands or putting their arms around each other. However, some of his warmest memories of growing up centered on his parents bringing him gifts. These gifts were not extravagant, but they reminded Roger that he was loved.

When Roger married Sally, he just assumed that buying her gifts would communicate that same message of love to her. He regularly brought home something special and presented it to her as a token of his love. He never understood why she seemed less than enthusiastic about his desire to show appreciation to her through gift-giving.

Sally was raised in a family that openly demonstrated affection. She grew up feeling most loved when someone touched her or communicated verbal words of affection. After she married Roger, she would ask him to hold her hand and put his arm around her. She wanted him to tell her how much he loved her. But Roger was disinterested in nonsexual touch and found it difficult to express himself verbally. Over time, Sally began to pull away from Roger.

Can you see how this couple could feel disconnected? Roger gave Sally gifts, which was what he liked to receive. Sally attempted to show love to Roger through talk and nonsexual touch, which was what she liked to receive. They were using the wrong love languages to communicate with each other. This left them feeling misunderstood and isolated. As Roger and Sally learned to speak each other's love language, their marital intimacy and ability to experience SOUL*gasm* dramatically increased.

Identifying the way your spouse receives love provides a key that opens the door to deeper intimacy. Jesus said, "A new commandment I give to you, that you love one another, even as I have loved you, that you also love one another. By this all men will know that you are My disciples, if you have love for one another."[14] The quality of a person's love for God, themselves, and their spouse is what distinguishes them from the world. Couples who invest in understanding each other's temperaments, likes/dislikes, and love languages advance in intimacy—and experience SOUL*gasms* more often.

Life is lived in a story

anne

In our own marriage, learning how to understand each other's tempera-ments, likes/dislikes, and giving and receiving love completely transformed the way we related to each other. Early in our marriage we wondered why our attempts to communicate love to each other often failed. I remember one spectacular failure in vivid detail.

It had been a really long week. I knew Tim would be on duty at the firehouse over the weekend, so I was looking forward to being home with the kids. But first I needed to do some grocery shopping and run a few errands. My sister came over to watch the kids, which allowed me to complete my to-do list in half the time.

As I finally headed for home, my mind began to drift. I imagined myself soaking in a hot bath, getting into my pajamas, and relaxing on the couch with the kids. I had even picked up a movie that we could enjoy watching together. As I pulled into the driveway, I should have guessed something was up when I saw the kids rushing out of the house. They seemed unusually excited to see me.

My sister met me at the car and told me that a "big surprise" was waiting for me in the house. I'm not a person who really enjoys surprises, but I obediently shut my eyes as the kids instructed, and allowed my giggling brood to lead me back to the bedroom.

"Okay, Mommy. Open your eyes!" they shouted. On the bed was an envelope with a single red rose lying next to it. I looked at my sister, confused and hoping for more information or some kind of explanation. The kids were shouting, "Read it, Mom, read it!" As I slowly opened the envelope, I recognized Tim's handwriting:

Surprise!

This red rose is just the beginning of a romantic weekend for two.

Don't worry about a thing. The kids are in good hands.

Don't worry about your clothes. I have a suitcase packed for you.

Just kiss everyone goodbye and head to the car.

Once you get inside, look in the glove compartment.

The kids were jumping up and down, clapping their hands and giggling. I know they expected me to share in their excitement, but I was too tired to feel their joy. My dreams of taking a hot bath and curling up on the couch were slipping away. I started firing off questions at my sister: "What's going on? I thought Tim was on duty at the firehouse. What is he up to? Where is he taking me? When did he write this note? What clothes did he pack? How long will we be gone?" None of my questions were answered, and it soon became obvious that no amount of begging would persuade my sister or children to turn informant.

In that moment, I was reminded of why I don't like surprises. I'm one of those people who looks around the house for my presents before Christmas. I have even been known to take a quick peek and rewrap them. When it's my birthday, I would prefer a gift certificate. That way I can pick out exactly what I want, rather than being surprised with things I don't really need. I began to think about the note Tim had written me—specifically the line that announced, "Don't worry about your clothes. I have a suitcase packed for you."

How could Tim possibly know what clothes to pack for me? Did he throw in my favorite jeans? Did he remember my makeup and blow dryer? A low-level panic began to set in as I remembered the last time Tim picked out an outfit for me, back when we were dating. He had wanted to surprise me for our first Christmas together. We were sitting with his family as I opened up the first box and pulled out a pair of size six pants—I wore a size ten. Tim assured me they would fit because the material was "stretchy"! The next box contained a matching poncho featuring a very distinct design. It looked a lot like a rug, which is fine if you are going for an Aztec look. The third box held the finale—something Tim assured me was a very special "accessory" to go with the Aztec rug-poncho and skin-tight pants. I was afraid to open it. I finally looked inside the box and found a burnt-orange, suede Ringo cap!

As you can see, my apprehension about Tim packing my clothes was rooted in painful experience. I checked my closet to see what was missing. My favorite pants were still on a hanger. As I took further inventory, I noticed the blouse that was missing was the one I could barely button since I started breastfeeding. Staring at an empty hanger, I realized the pants he had chosen were the ones I kept in my closet to remind me of my "goal weight."

However, since I was working at becoming a more *fun* person, I needed to fight my natural tendency to default to party-pooper mode. Determined to play along, I followed Tim's instructions and headed back to the car. Sure enough, envelope number two was inside the glove compartment. It read:

> *Let the games begin ... It's time to party!*
>
> *Back out of the driveway and head to Schaumburg Fire Station #1.*
>
> *When you arrive, park in the side lot and walk inside.*
>
> *Have fun!*

The thought of walking into an unknown situation at the firehouse was a bit unnerving. But I remember thinking that the faster I cooperated, the sooner this game would be over. When I walked into the firehouse, the firemen began teasing me about "the great adventure" Tim had planned. I tried to get some information from them, but no one was talking. They told me if I wanted the next envelope, I would have to slide down the fire pole!

Now, I've never considered myself to be a pole-type of girl! But I know from experience that if a person shows any weakness to firemen, it only adds to the teasing. So I pretended to laugh and enjoy the process as I climbed the staircase to the second floor. Did I mention that I'm afraid of heights? Nevertheless, I wrapped my arms and legs around the pole and slid down. I hit the ground a lot harder than I expected. They said, "Nice job, Annie," and handed me envelope number three. It read:

> *Way to go! Mission accomplished.*
>
> *Let's see, what's next?*
>
> *Drive east on Schaumburg Road. Head north on Meacham Road.*
>
> *East on Golf Road. Pull into Houlihan's parking lot.*
>
> *Walk up to the bar and ask to talk to Tommy the bartender.*
>
> *He will give you envelope #4.*

After my little trip down the fire pole in front of Tim's coworkers, I was not in the mood for any more "fun." I could feel the blood rushing through my veins as my blood pressure shot up. At this point, I was so angry I just wanted to go home. But I pressed on, determined to be a good sport. I walked into the restaurant, asked for Tommy the bartender, who was more than willing to give me the envelope—but only after I sang a little Irish song.

Once I actually got the envelope, I noticed it had some coins taped inside to a note that read:

You are getting closer.

There is a pay phone outside.

Use this change to dial the number below.

I walked outside, located the pay phone, inserted the coins, and dialed the number. Tim picked up on the first ring and greeted me in his romantic voice. He told me to look across the parking lot toward the hotel on the other side of the road. As I looked in that direction, I saw Tim in the window of a hotel room. He was dancing, waving enthusiastically, and blowing me kisses. He was having a wonderful time! Before I could blurt out a word, he said, "Head up to room 444 ... I'll be waiting for you. We have the honeymoon suite for the entire weekend—*let the love-fest begin!*"

I was so angry I don't even remember driving across the busy street. I vaguely recall parking the car and taking the elevator upstairs. I stomped down the hallway toward our room. Surely my footsteps were shaking the very foundations of the building. I scanned the room numbers and saw the door to room 444 ajar. I pushed it open. The room was dark, and soft music was playing in the background. A path of rose petals covered the floor. (A side note: I later found out that Tim had stopped by to see his friend at the funeral home down the street to pick up a few dozen "used roses" from the last visitation!) Following the flowery pathway into a candlelit bathroom, I found Tim soaking in a tub full of bubbles. He looked *so* relaxed. His eyes were closed and he had a huge smile on his face.

All I could think of was, *I want to drown him!*

+ + +

Somehow our marriage survived this *weekend from hell,* but we had much to learn about the differences in our temperaments, likes/dislikes, and how to speak each other's love language. Unlike me, Tim loves surprises. What would have been a great SOUL*gasm* adventure for him was a total disaster for me. I would have loved to have known about our getaway weeks in advance. With four small kids at home, I would have enjoyed anticipating and planning for our romantic getaway. I would have gotten some rest and packed my own clothes. But to go from grocery shopping after a long, stressful day, to visiting the firehouse, to sliding down a fire pole, to visiting a bar, to singing a song for a total stranger, to then walking into a hotel room and seeing Tim all revved up for a romantic weekend … well, let's just say it was more than I could handle.

This was an invitation early in our marriage to invest in purposefully growing in intimacy—in knowing and being fully known. Back then we couldn't even define intimacy, let alone understand how two people could maintain their individual identities and joyfully embrace each other's differences.

In marriage, understanding a spouse's gifts, temperaments, love languages, and styles of relating takes time. And as the story of our UN-romantic weekend shows, differences often lead to conflict. People who are conflict avoiders may not be comfortable verbally responding to a situation imme-diately. They may need more time to process. Days later they may think to themselves, *I should have said this* or *I should have said that*. Others who lean toward a more aggressive style of relating may view conflict and confrontation as opportunities to gain clarity on a subject. Knowing both the positive and negative aspects of how you and your spouse are wired is vital to advancing in intimacy. This knowledge becomes the pathway to experiencing SOUL*gasm*.

CHOOSING YOUR MODEL FOR MARRIAGE

God created every person with the freedom and ability to make choices. You are free to choose whom you will marry, who you will serve, and whose authority you will submit to. You can choose to submit to God, the Enemy, or others. Every married couple is also free to choose what their marriage view will be and how they will walk it out. Because Jesus took back dominion and authority from Satan, we believe husbands and wives are free to return to the marriage principles of Paradise.

We love to challenge couples to revisit God's creational marriage design. Of course, we understand that a couple's marriage view is not an issue of salvation. But every married couple is free to choose to live out tra-ditional, hierarchical, complementarian, or egalitarian marriage views. Personally, we are totally committed to wholeheartedly living out God's "in the beginning," creational, co-leadership marriage design.

Take some time and review Genesis chapters 1 and 2. Study how mar-riage was originally designed. *In the beginning*—before sin entered the story—we do not find any evidence of headship, hierarchy, female sub-ordination, or the husband designated as the head (the wife's cover or spiritual leader). In the beginning, the husband and wife lived in mutual equality (intrinsically and functionally); *both* the man and woman were made in God's image.[15] They enjoyed mutual authority; *both* were given the procreation and dominion (rulership) mandates.[16] Reclaiming and living out the mutuality principles of Paradise will impact not only you and your marriage, but also your children, grandchildren, the church, our culture, and future generations.[17]

We challenge couples to give co-leadership a try, agree for three months that you will only make decisions in unity. This includes both of you **I.O.T.L.** and waiting until you both have "green lights" from God before you pull the trigger on a decision. Record what happens; we believe you will be surprised by how co-leading together—without specific pre-designated restrictions or roles—will provide you with power and protection. And as you focus on being reciprocal servants and functional equals, your intimacy and opportunities for SOUL*gasm* moments will dramatically increase.

Life is lived in a story

tim

STAY IN YOUR LANE!

Over the years, the two of us have become all too familiar with the good and bad parts of each other's temperaments and styles of relating. One of the negative things about my temperament is that I can tend to be controlling. Truth be told, I like to be in charge. This plays out in many ways. For example, when we were leading a Tim + Anne REAL LIFE Marriage Advance in New York, the couple running point for the gathering offered to purchase donuts for the set-up team. On the way to the church we pulled into a drive-through lane, and the driver casually ordered "two dozen assorted donuts." Sitting in the back of the van, I grew tense as I thought: *Doesn't she know that ordering "assorted donuts" is code for the person to give you the donuts no one else wants, the stale ones that have been on the shelf two days, and the ones they dropped on the floor and returned to the tray? When a person orders donuts, they must be in total control and select each donut by name.*

In years past when Anne tried to point out some area where I was being too controlling, it never seemed to be the right time for me to hear her. I often felt attacked, disrespected, or misunderstood. As a result, the conversation would almost inevitably end poorly. One day Anne took me on a date to one of my favorite restaurants. After a great meal and lots of good conversation, she began to talk about our marriage. I was all ears as she started listing things she loved and respected about me. She even mentioned some specific things she had recently noticed. Then she said, "Hon, I'm so thankful for you, but there is one little thing I want to talk with you about. It's about our *different styles of relating.*"

Uh-oh. I have known Anne almost my entire life, and we've been down this road more times than I can count. Based on past experience, I interpreted the phrase "styles of relating" as code for "Tim, you might think you are a low-maintenance, strong-leader-type guy, but you can often morph into a more high-maintenance, controlling-type guy!"

But this time, Anne took the conversation in a new direction. Instead of hitting me with a verbal two-by-four, Anne gently made some observations about my style of relating. I listened to what she had to say. Although part of me wanted to defend myself, I knew in my heart that she was speaking truth to me in love. In her winsome way, Anne used a story to make her point. She reminded me of how much I love to drive. And she was right. I love driving cars, trucks, motorcycles, anything with wheels.

As a firefighter, I drove the hook-and-ladder for ten years. I probably love driving because when I'm driving—you guessed it—I'm in control. Knowing my love for driving, Anne asked me a question: "Have you ever been driving along the highway, just enjoying your day, when someone suddenly pulls into your lane and cuts you off?"

I replied, "Oh yeah, I can't stand being cut off."

Anne said, "Hon, I want to say this in love, but at times in our marriage, I feel I am in the driver's seat. I have a plan. I know what I'm doing and where I'm going. Then you walk into the house and it feels like you swerve into my lane and cut me off. I know you're not trying to take the steering wheel out of my hands, but it often feels that way to me. I really don't want to keep arguing about this or continue to try to defend my position. I suspect you don't see this as a control issue. But in the future when this happens, how about if I gently remind you of this conversation by simply asking you to 'stay in your lane'?"

Anne's "stay-in-your-lane" illustration hit the bull's eye. I understood her example of being cut off. I could see how my desire to lead could have a negative effect on her. As I look back now, if she had said, "Tim, you are one of the most controlling people I know," I would have responded defensively. And in a matter of minutes, things would have quickly gone south. However, her words were life-giving. She spoke truth in love. I did not feel disrespected or parented. I apologized and asked her for forgiveness. More important, I made a commitment to work on "staying in my lane."

That simple slogan, *"Stay in your lane,"* has served us well over the years. We use it often to gain perspective and defuse potential misunderstandings. In fact, when the "assorted donuts" were being ordered at the drive-through window, Anne leaned over and whispered to me, "Hon, stay in your lane!"

ADVANCING IN SOUL*GASM*

In marriage, God invites a husband and wife to deeper levels of intimacy, and more wholehearted living. Strategic steps to advance in intimacy include learning a spouse's (and your own) spiritual gifts, temperament, love languages, behaviors, mannerisms, character traits, likes/dislikes, strengths, and weaknesses. And as husbands and wives choose to appreciate their spouse's unique design, rather than letting it become a divisive issue, this opens the door to co-leading together, celebrating *ordinary* and *extraordinary* moments, and experiencing SOUL*gasm*.

CHAPTER 4

DISTINGUISHING BETWEEN
ROLES AND FUNCTIONS

Whenever we counsel couples or lead workshops, there are certain topics that are sure to surface—*roles* in marriage is one of them. Using terms without understanding what they mean can become confusing. So let's kick off this chapter by asking a few questions to get some perspective on this topic: *What is your role as a wife? How do you function as a wife? What is your role as a husband? How do you function as a husband? How do you function as a couple?*

Roles and *functions* are such important topics that we touched on them in our book *NAKED* and decided to devote an entire chapter addressing them here. *Why?* Because *how* a husband and wife understand and live out perceptions surrounding *roles* and *functions* directly impacts the intimacy they share. It also impacts how they understand what it means for a husband and wife to "become one"[1] and to "rule" together in unity.[2]

ROLES

The response to a man or women's *role* is often seen through a cultural lens rather than from a biblical perspective. The primary *role* for every follower

of Christ, both men and women, is to live out the Great Commandment—
love.[3] In marriage, a husband and wife are invited to focus on the *role* of
being a servant. The Bible says, "The greatest among you will be your
servant."[4] This includes loving and serving a spouse *through good times
and bad, in sickness and health, until death parts them*. Philippians 2:3-4
(NIV) says, "Do nothing out of selfish ambition or vain conceit. Rather,
in humility value others above yourselves, not looking to your own interests but each of you to the interests of the others."

Every husband and wife can take ownership and responsibility to walk
together as co-leaders and reciprocal servants, and *function* in the gifts
God has given each of them—without restrictions. This involves understanding each other, and prayerfully deciding what works best in their
marriage. Of course, this looks different for different couples. A worthy
goal for couples is to celebrate unity, mutuality, and diversity, rather
than trying to force each other into predetermined *roles* solely based
on gender.

Concerning *roles*, many people believe men/husbands are required by
God to step into the *role* of being God's designated leader. However,
before the fall, God commanded *both* the man and woman to rule
together.[5] Plus, the reality is that God has given many wives stronger
leadership gifts than their husbands. And in our counseling experiences,
we've seen many husbands who have been given strong leadership gifts
fail to purposefully include their wives. When this takes place, God's
desire for a couple to "co-lead and co-serve as co-equals in Christ"[6] gets
compromised. And this negatively impacts soul connection, and *blocks*
opportunities for couples to experience SOUL*gasm* moments.

We meet other men/husbands who do not have strong leadership gifts.
They can easily get discouraged when they fail to meet the traditional

religious gender *roles* and expectations that the church culture has put in place. On other occasions, we've counseled wives who are dissatisfied with what they perceive as their husband not fulfilling his *role* surrounding spiritual leadership. And even church leaders can default to overemphasizing—at times shaming—husbands. Many church leaders directly and indirectly communicate to husbands that they are not leading strong enough, praying hard enough, parenting well enough, managing the finances, or providing the "spiritual cover" they are supposed to provide.

Many husbands respond with frustration, anger, or fear; or they default to active or passive control. Their control typically relates to traditional-hierarchical-complementarian authority perspectives that are taught by the majority of churches. And it's been our experience that this often results in discounting and disrespecting wives; and in extreme cases, dominating, or even abusing them. Other husbands default to deserting as they check out emotionally, physically, and spiritually. Tragically, some husbands just give up. We've met with husbands who say they have reached the conclusion that *I'll never be able to successfully live out the spiritual leader role that my wife wants and church leaders say I'm supposed to be—so why bother?* And they invest their time and energy in other interests.

For example, we have a good friend who has incredible service gifts, and his wife has amazing leadership gifts. He has told us on a number of occasions that at home, things work smoothly. But in the church, he experiences shame as leaders convey—subtly and not so subtly—that he "needs to *man up* and step into his God-ordained role as the spiritual leader in his marriage." He also describes how church leaders have conveyed—subtly and not so subtly—to him that his strong, gifted wife "is coming on too strong and needs to tone it down a bit."

MASCULINITY AND THE "MANLY MAN"

Regarding *roles* and *functions*, the narrative established throughout history portrays a "manly man" as a macho man who typically treats women poorly, drinks hard, is quick to fight, and takes no prisoners. Add to the typical "man's man" portrayal a measure of male insecurity, shame-fear-control, centuries of misogyny, hierarchy, as well as an overall misunderstanding of true biblical manhood, and this can become a male-gender recipe for disaster. And sadly, women are often the first to be impacted by the negative fallout. In addition, there are other factors, including family of origin, culture, environment, and seasons of history that play into "man's man" views and perceptions.

For example, a "man's man" in the Western United States a century ago was the man who rode a horse all day, handled guns well, had sex with multiple women, smoked tobacco, and drank lots of whiskey. A "man's man" in the sports world is typically the man who runs the fastest, jumps the highest, and is the strongest and toughest. Then stop and consider how Hollywood typically portrays a "man's man." In the mid-1970s when Tim began his career with the fire department, before firefighters used self-contained breathing apparatuses, the "man's man" was the fireman who could inhale the most smoke. Called a "leather-lunger," he was the man young firefighters looked up to. Sadly, most leather-lungers died early from lung cancer.

It's important to remember that masculine characteristics come in many different variations. For example, during World War II, were the infantry soldiers who stormed the beaches at Normandy any manlier than J. Robert Oppenheimer and his colleagues who developed the Atomic bomb? Looking back, we wonder: *Which of these groups of men made a greater impact on history?*

Another example, consider Caesar the emperor of Rome who ruled with an iron fist. Compare him to John the Baptist who lived a celibate life in the wilderness and wore clothes made of camel's hair. His food included locusts and wild honey, and his mission was preaching, "Repent, for the kingdom of heaven is at hand."[7] Can we ask, *Do you think Caesar or John was greater—and the more "manly man"?* Jesus answered that question, saying, "Truly I tell you, among those born of women there has not risen anyone greater than John the Baptist; yet whoever is least in the kingdom of heaven is greater than he."[8]

In addition to the historical and cultural masculine narrative, the feminine narrative established throughout history typically portrays a woman as a princess, a sex object for men's pleasure, or a damsel in distress who needs to be rescued by a strong man. However, it's interesting that the first rescue recorded in the Bible was by a *woman*. Review the story, it was the woman (*Ezer*) who rescued the man from his "not good" condition of aloneness.[9] *Ezer* is such a strong, Hebrew word. It means "warrior, strength, savior, power, and protector." In fact, God is often portrayed as an *Ezer*—"the Lord is a warrior [*Ezer*]; the Lord is His Name."[10]

Life is lived in a story

tim

I believe it would be wise to revisit what a "man's man" truly is. For example, I grew up in a family with five males (my dad and four boys); as well as my mom and sister. Dad was a hard-working, union-card-carrying milkman. He was a great athlete, a decorated World War II soldier, and a Golden Gloves boxing champion. After a twenty-plus-year career in the fire service, I retired as deputy fire chief from a department that included one hundred and fifty men (no women were firefighters at that time). I also have a lifetime of local church and parachurch experiences. All that is to say, I think I understand the classic, stereotypical Alpha male, macho, man-up, "man's man" characterization. However, at this season in my life, I believe the "man's man" portrayal—one I've found in most churches and men's ministries—is more often than not a mixed bag.

My experience has been that the "man's man" mantra typically includes high *machismo*—defined as "an exaggerated sense or display of masculinity, emphasizing characteristics that are conventionally regarded as male, usually physical strength and courage, aggressiveness, and lack of emotional response."[11] As a side note, for men who have experienced a Christian men's retreat, you may have noticed the inordinate number of Alpha males wearing combat camouflage, and the uber use of military language. Hanging around men for more than sixty years, my real-life experience has taught me that not all men are Alpha males, nor were they created to be. And my take is that many men's leaders are repackaging the traditional, stereotypical, masculine, macho, man-up, gender-essentialism narrative that has reverberated for centuries.

Personally, instead of being known as a "man's man" in the ways it's stereotypically described, I would prefer to be known as a man who loved God with all my heart, soul, mind, and strength; a one-woman man who passionately loved my bride well my entire lifetime; a man who captured the hearts of my wife, kids, and grandkids; and a man who was a faithful friend. I'd like to be known as a man who lived wholeheartedly, shed godly tears, prayed passionate prayers, and when I came to a crossroads in life, by God's grace, I chose the more difficult path.

Anne and I understand that for many years, church leaders have told men they are God's designated leaders. And if they got married, they would have authority over their wife, and were required to be the leader and provide a "spiritual cover" over her. Scholars can endlessly argue a handful of controversial Bible passages. However, *in the beginning*, we don't see any evidence of inequality, hierarchy, headship, designated male leadership, female subordination, or the husband labeled as the wife's leader or "spiritual cover." Review the text; *none* of these were present in God's creational marriage design before sin entered the marriage story.

It concerns me when male religious leaders confidently declare that the real key to kingdom-of-God advancement is for husbands to step up, man up, and become a "man's man." Certainly, husbands stepping into their true identities and initiating more in marriage and relationships will bring a measure of kingdom-of-God advancement. However, in my opinion, the kingdom of God will advance more successfully if husbands focus on their true identities and live out how God uniquely wired and gifted them. And then celebrate and fully embrace the God-given strengths in their wives (and women), as they encourage them to step into their pre-fall, *Ezer* calling. Unfortunately, when it comes to many local church and parachurch ministries, the Enemy has, in effect, cunningly neutralized half the church and half of marriages; and the powerhouse in husband-wife mutuality and co-leadership has been compromised.

GOD IS NOT A MAN

It is important when talking about *roles* and *functions* to understand that "God is not a man."[12] God's essence transcends sexuality and gender and includes both masculine and feminine characteristics. The Bible says that "God is a spirit."[13]

There are texts in the Bible that focus more on stereotypical masculine characteristics: "The LORD is a warrior; the LORD is His Name."[14] And there are texts that describe more stereotypical, feminine-like characteristics, such as comforting and merciful: "Blessed be the God and Father of our Lord Jesus Christ, the Father of mercies and God of all comfort; who comforts us in our affliction so that we may be able to comfort those who are in any affliction with which we ourselves are comforted by God."[15]

And the apostle Paul—a true man's man—wrote to the church in Thessalonica, saying, "We proved to be gentle among you, as a nursing mother tenderly cares for her own children. Having thus a fond affection for you...."[16] Re-read that passage. The apostle Paul, the man who under the inspiration of the Holy Spirit wrote the majority of the New Testament, described early Christ-followers' behaviors as being like a *gentle and nursing mother*. Can we ask, *Would you describe the apostle Paul and early Christ-followers as "nursing mothers"?*

HOW DID JESUS DESCRIBE HIMSELF?

Let's pause to review the life of Jesus. He modeled a full range of feelings and life experiences. He lived a life of adventure—rebuking storms, healing people, bringing the dead back to life. Jesus also engaged in battles—after His baptism, Jesus was led by the Holy Spirit into the wilderness for a power encounter with Satan. Throughout His life, Jesus regularly engaged in spiritual battles with demons and verbal battles with religious and political leaders.

Jesus experienced a full range of emotions, including sadness, anger, fear, happiness, excitement, and tenderness. He modeled love, humility, gentleness, and compassion. He treated women with unheard-of honor and respect. He embraced children, spoke lovingly to outcasts, washed men's feet, and openly wept. All that is to say, if you described Jesus, what words would you use? Most people respond by saying, "Jesus is the

Savior, Lord, and Lion of Judah. He's a strong *warrior;* He had supernatural *power*," and so on.

We agree with all of those descriptions of Jesus. And many of the above words used to describe Jesus are strikingly similar to the meaning of God's designation of the first *woman (remember, Ezer* means "warrior, strength, savior, power, and protector"). Nonetheless, there is only one time in the Bible when Jesus described Himself; He said, "I am gentle and humble in heart."[17] Stop for a moment and consider: Are *gentleness* and *humility* words that you would use to describe Jesus, or other passionate, brave-hearted men?

We encourage people to thoughtfully evaluate popular messages about the masculine/feminine gender-essentialism cultural narrative that absolutizes masculinity, femininity, and gender *roles*. While we may resonate with some of the writings on these subjects, we offer for your consideration a non-traditional, non-gender-essentialism perspective that includes mutuality and functional equality.

MEN AND WOMEN ARE DIFFERENT

Every person is created as a unique, one-of-a-kind man or woman. Their differences reflect God's plurality and creative design. That said, it's important to remember that *differences are not better or worse, differences are good*.

In marriage, we encourage husbands and wives not to focus on differences, but instead focus on *unconditional love*. We define unconditional love as loving a spouse without expecting anything in return. And this becomes the pathway for a husband/wife to Reflect and Reveal the heart of God to their spouse. Practically speaking, this includes living in the

Larger Story and declaring through actions and attitudes that *marriage is not about me.* Our experience is that these behaviors open the door for couples to advance in intimacy and to experience SOUL*gasm.*

We suspect some readers may be thinking, *But men and women are so different.* Remember, differences-variety-diversity are good. And differences between husbands and wives vary from individual to individual, and from couple to couple. That said, there are more similarities between men and women than there are differences. God created every person as a unique human being made in His image.[18] And any differences between women and men should be celebrated. They should never be used to restrict or control.

FUNCTIONS

It's been our experience that when a person focuses on predetermined *roles* based on gender, it can lead to all sorts of intimacy *blocking* issues. These include confusion, control, competition, and unrighteous judgment. That is why instead of emphasizing *roles*, we prefer to use the term *functions.* For example, there are times in the counseling aspect of REAL LIFE Ministries where Anne *functions* more in a leadership capacity—so she leads. And there are times when we lead REAL LIFE marriage gatherings where Tim *functions* more in a leadership capacity—then he leads.

Our desire is to maximize the gifts God has given *both* of us. For example, God has given Anne amazing wisdom, discernment, counseling, and teaching gifts. And He has given Tim gifts of faith, encouragement, leadership, and prayer. In our marriage, we focus on maximizing *all* our gifts, and we *function* without predetermined *roles* that are supposed to be played out in specific ways solely based on gender. That is why we avoid using the term *roles,* because it can lead to focusing on cultural expectations of men and women.

Practically speaking, we make it a top marriage priority to implement the **Traffic Light Principle.** This involves purposefully putting God first. He is the one we want to lead our decision-making process. We *function* best in this way, rather than making decisions based on who is male, who is female, or who has a specific predetermined *role.* We start by **I.O.T.L.** and we have agreed to only make decisions when we *both* sense "green lights" from God. Our emphasis is to love and serve God and each other. And as we look back over forty-plus years of marriage, we believe co-leading in unity and focusing on *functions* based on gifts, has provided us with immeasurable power and protection.

When we teach about using *functions* instead of *roles,* we are often asked, "But who is the *leader* in your marriage, isn't it supposed to be the man, the husband?" We respond by explaining that the leader in our marriage is Jesus. We sincerely believe the best leaders are the best followers. Jesus, the quintessential servant-leader, said, "Follow Me."[19] Our top priority is focusing on following Jesus and then co-leading—*together.* And as we do this, in only God fashion, it increases our oneness, intimacy, our opportunity for celebrating *ordinary* and *extraordinary* moments—and our moments of experiencing SOUL*gasm.*

As we conclude this chapter, we want to clarify that we know this can seem like radical thinking to some. To others, perhaps it comes with a fresh sense of hope and change. Often, after we teach about *roles, functions,* and God's co-leadership creational marriage design, a man will approach us, shake his head back and forth, and say, "But God is a God of order, someone has to wear the pants in the family—and that person should be the *man*—the *husband*—*me!*"

We smile and respond, "After decades of marriage, we have reached the conclusion that how a husband and wife live out *roles* and *functions* directly relates to advancing in oneness, intimacy, and experiencing SOUL*gasm*. And as for us and our marriage, we function best—and by far have the most fun—when neither of us wears any pants!"

CHAPTER 5

LIVING OUT LOVE AND RESPECT

We have always made it a priority to attend marriage conferences every year. Not only are we committed to growing in our own marriage and spiritual formation, but as co-leaders of REAL LIFE Ministries, we want to stay current with what is available to couples.

When we first moved to Colorado Springs, we were invited to attend a marriage conference called *Love and Respect*.[1] We quickly realized that the primary focus of this conference was based on a specific Ephesians Bible text: "Nevertheless, each individual among you also is to *love* his own wife even as himself, and the wife must *see to it* that she *respects* her husband."[2]

That same marriage conference has returned to Colorado Springs a number of times. That said, we can always recognize when a *Love and Respect* conference is held in our region. *Why?* Because after the conference leaves town, we get multiple requests for counseling. And throughout decades of counseling, we've seen that it's typically *wives* who call to schedule appointments. However, after a *Love and Respect* conference, it's the *husbands* who make the appointments.

Note: The following story is a typical conversation we've had with couples who have heard the *Love and Respect* message. We will refer to the clients in this story as "Joe and Jane."[3]

Life is lived in a story

tim+anne

Joe begins with a measure of confident enthusiasm, "Tim, after attending the *Love and Respect* conference, I was reminded that the best way to walk out my marriage is not all that complicated. For me, as the husband, it's my job to *love* my wife; and it's my wife's job to *respect* me."

Joe goes on to paraphrase the Bible verse he heard repeatedly quoted at the conference, "'A husband must *love* his wife as he loves himself, and the wife must *respect* her husband.'[4] Tim, this love-and-respect Bible text is *crystal clear!*"

[Sidebar, I (Anne) have observed over the years that when a conversation like this is taking place, the man is usually talking to Tim and giving him direct eye contact. Even though the conversation is between all four of us, the husband's conversation is directed to Tim.]

Tim responded, "Joe, I'm familiar with that unique and one-of-a-kind short passage, but let's take a step back and look throughout the Scriptures. *Both* husbands and wives are created to love and be loved. In fact, the passage you just quoted says a husband must love his wife as he *loves himself*. Seems to me it's *crystal clear* that love is important to husbands—beginning with self-love. In fact, Jesus summed up the entire Law and the Prophets with what has become known as the Great Commandment: to *love* God, *love* our neighbors, and *love* ourselves.[5] *Love* is the primary goal for *both* husbands and wives—for *all* Christ-followers. The apostle Paul wrote to the church in Corinth and declared: 'And yet I will show you the most excellent way'[6]—the way of *love*. Then he wrote what has become known as the love chapter, saying, 'And now these three remain: faith, hope, and *love. But the greatest of these is love.*'"[7]

Joe interrupted, "But every husband needs *respect!*"

Tim asked, "Joe, are you saying you believe that love and respect are gender exclusive?"

Joe shook his head back and forth and said, "I'm not sure."

Tim continued, "First Peter 3:7 says that husbands are commanded to grant their wives *honor* as a fellow heir of the grace of life. Honor and respect go hand in hand; the Bible commands the wife to *respect* her husband, and the husband to *honor* his wife as a fellow heir. Let's look at another passage in Hebrews that reads, 'Marriage *is to be held* in honor among all.'[8] In addition to a wife respecting her husband, Titus 2:4 says that wives are also to 'love their husbands.' These passages illuminate the oneness, intimacy, and co-leadership unique to marriage. Joe, can I ask you a question?"

"Sure."

"Looking at the life of Jesus Christ, do you think He focused more on *love* or *respect*?"

Joe slowly replied, "I'm not sure."

"Joe, as I read the Word, I don't see Jesus saying that *respect* was the key to His personal fulfillment, longings, or desires. And He never instructed His disciples or followers to *respect* Him. Throughout Jesus' life, He was both tough and tender—warrior and prophet—depending on the circumstances. In the book of John, after Jesus' death and resurrection, He was preparing a meal for Peter, one of His closest friends. Remember that before Jesus' crucifixion, Peter denied Jesus three times. The Bible describes how the resurrected Christ asked Peter three times, 'Do you *love* Me?'[9] It's interesting to note that Jesus did not ask Peter, 'Do you *respect* Me?' Jesus understood the transforming power of love in the heart and life of a man. And He knew that love—not respect—lasts forever."

Joe responded, "But, Tim, let's go back to the Ephesians passage—it commands a wife to *respect* her husband."

"Joe, it does say that, but to overemphasize *respect* for men leads to deemphasizing *respect* for women. Think about this: A person cannot *love* without committing to the valuing that love entails. Recognizing value in another person is foundational to *respect*. But a person can *respect* without *loving*. For example, in the fire department a firefighter is required to *respect* a fire officer because of that person's rank. However, they are not required to *love* the officer. Likewise, a wife can respect her husband without loving him. However, it's impossible to love without respecting because respect is one of the necessary ingredients of love."

Joe responded, "But the love-and-respect marriage message is so popular."

Tim replied, "I agree, it is a popular message in the church-world. But our experience has been that popular messages can often take on a life of their own. Husbands regularly come into our counseling office, describing to us how they are convinced the major problem in their marriage is that their wives do not give them the *respect* the Bible commands—*and they deserve!* Unfortunately, it seldom crosses their minds that their marriage problems could relate to their own selfishness, family-of-origin issues, destructive hierarchical positions, shame, control, rebellion, rejection, or the choice to live in the smaller story—where *it's all about me.*"

Joe replied, "So, are you saying you disagree with love-and-respect principles?"

"No, as a matter of fact, Anne and I have personally implemented some of the love-and-respect principles. But we have determined that a healthy, life-giving, kingdom-advancing marriage is much more than a husband focusing on *love* and a wife focusing on *respect*. Marriage is not that simple; intimate relationships are complex."

Joe asked, "Tim, can you give me a love-and-respect example from your life?"

Tim answered, "I'll try. I remember a time early in our marriage when I was disrespectful to Anne in a major way. Anne had told me about something that happened to her that was funny to me, but embarrassed her. That weekend we were driving to a firefighters' party, and on our way, she looked me directly in the eyes and told me she did *not* want me to share what had happened to her. I promised not to tell the story—even though it was hilarious.

"Firefighters' parties are filled with lots of fun, food, and cold beverages. As the night progressed, I shared with some firemen the story that Anne asked me not to share. When she overheard me telling the story, she was obviously angry. On the drive home, she told me how disrespectful and discounting my behavior was, and how not keeping my promise made her angry, and *blocked* her from trusting that I would keep my word.

"When we got home, I looked her in her eyes and told her I was sorry. I explained that I was wrong for telling the story. And I was wrong for disrespecting her, embarrassing her, and not keeping my promise. However, I understood that my verbal apology meant very little without a change in my behavior. I became determined to rebuild the trust that was broken. And I made it a priority to show Anne *respect* by honoring her—and my personal goal was to return to being a 'man of my word.'

"Over the next few months I met with my mentor. I wanted to understand *why* I was placing what I wanted over what I promised Anne. And at home, I looked for every opportunity to model respect to Anne through my behavior and by keeping my word. Through wise counsel and inner healing, I began to better understand some of my insecurities and family-of-origin propensities—in this specific instance, wanting to be the life of the party. A main focus for me became making certain that my *yes* was *yes* and my *no* was *no*. Slowly, over time, trust was restored. Looking back, one piece of gold I came away with was realizing that as much as Anne enjoyed when I showed her *love*, I also needed to make it a top priority to show her *respect*."

Tim continued, "We enjoy leading small groups of 'co-leadership communities.' And when our topic is love and respect, we ask the wives in our group if they prefer their husbands show *love* or *respect* to them. The overwhelming majority of women say they prefer their husbands show *respect* to them. And when we teach about love and respect at REAL LIFE marriage gatherings, we challenge wives to ask their husbands, 'Do you feel *loved* and *respected* by me?' And we challenge husbands to ask their wives, 'Do you feel *loved* and *respected* by me?' A husband or wife giving their spouse an opportunity to share his or her heart is an invitation to advance in intimacy—and experience SOUL*gasm*.

"Remember, God's creational marriage design includes mutuality and co-leadership. A husband and wife are *both* made in the image of God—the *imago Dei*. Within a plurality of persons—male and female—a couple is invited to Reflect and Reveal the diversity within the plurality of the Godhead. This includes 'co-leading, and co-serving, as co-equals in Christ.'"[10]

"But how does that play out in real life?" Joe asked.

Anne interrupted the dialogue Joe was having with Tim and said, "Joe, we've found that church culture, for the most part, understands the concept of love. However, husbands and wives tend to make respect contingent on a person's behavior. Spouses believe their husband or wife must earn respect, and they withhold it until their spouse behaves in the specific ways they deem acceptable."

Joe asked, "Are you saying I am supposed to love and respect Jane—no matter what?"

Anne responded, "Joe, that's a good question. It's important to clarify: We are not saying someone is commanded to love and respect his or her spouse's poor behavior. For example, a wife may not love and respect the behavior of a husband who continually acts out in narcissistic ways. But she can still treat him with love and respect. Likewise, a husband may not love and respect the behavior of a wife who makes unwise, self-centered decisions. But he can still treat her with love and respect. Our experience is that whether a spouse is treasured and honored more through love or respect—no matter how long a couple has been married—encouragement, affirmation, and presupposing the best in each other never get old. And concerning a spouse in an abusive relationship, a number of important factors come into play, including safety, appropriately dealing with abusive behavior, if necessary notifying the proper authorities, and in some cases, agreeing to a separation with the hope that the abusive spouse will seek healing and counsel, and the marriage can be restored."

Joe said, "Okay, I'm beginning to see that love and respect are not gender specific. But can you suggest any tools, or next steps, to help me advance in intimacy—in knowing my wife and being more fully known by her—and to help us experience more SOUL*gasm* moments?"

+ + +

GOALS AND DESIRES

These two important words can change the way a couple relates to one another. Understanding them can also serve as an effective tool to help live out many of the topics we've covered. Being equipped to differentiate between *goals* and *desires* can transform the way you interact regarding *roles* and *functions*, and *love* and *respect*. It can also help couples advance in intimacy and experience more SOUL*gasms*.

Let's start by defining these words so we are all on the same page. We define a *goal* and a *desire* differently. A goal is something a person can accomplish all by themselves; it does not require the participation of another person. For example, a goal could include daily prayer, regular exercise, or calling-texting-writing an encouraging note to someone. Remember, goals do *not* require the involvement of anyone else.

We define a *desire* as something a person wants to happen, but it requires the participation of others. For example, a desire could include having a great marriage and dynamic sex life; seeing your children and grandchildren loving God; having great friends; being part of a lively community of faith and seeing women treated in the church, and in our culture, with full functional equality. Each of these desires requires the involvement of others.

Life is lived in a story

tim

I have always been a goal-orientated person. Goals enable me to track my progress and make any necessary adjustments. Following are a number of *goals* I have:

+ To live out the Bible command to "clothe yourselves with humility toward one another."[11] Every day I ask God to enable me to choose humility over selfishness, envy, and pride.
+ To take ownership and responsibility for putting away childish things.[12] Often when I experience trouble, the bottom line for me—in one way or another—is that I need to *grow up!*
+ Additional goals include regular contact with my kids and grandkids, practicing the discipline of writing every day, reading a chapter of something every day (*leaders are readers*), exercising five times a week, and eating healthier (okay, that's a tough one!).

Note: None of these *goals* require the involvement of others.

Following are a number of *desires* I have surrounding my relationship with God:

+ I desire for God to help me see others in the ways He sees them, and to see myself in the ways my good Father sees me.
+ I desire to advance in intimacy with God—to better know Him and be better known by Him.

Note: Each of these *desires* require the involvement of others.

I have additional *desires* surrounding my marriage:

+ I desire to advance in oneness and intimacy with Anne.
+ I desire that Anne and I advance in living out what it means for "two to become one,"[13] and in living out God's description of the first married couple—*before* sin entered the story.
+ I desire that Anne and I advance in spiritual + emotional + physical (sexual) intimacy. Frankly, the physical/sexual part of God's naked without shame—removing clothes and getting naked—is not rocket science. It's more challenging to advance in emotional naked-ness—removing emotional fig leaves from my heart and life—connecting emotionally and experiencing SOUL*gasm* with my bride.

Note: Each of these desires require the involvement of Anne.

A few *desires* I have surrounding others includes:

+ I desire our children and grandchildren to passionately love God, and to be kind to themselves and others.
+ I desire to stay connected to my spiritual mentors.
+ I desire that our marriage books [*TOGETHER, NAKED,* SOUL*gasm*] positively impact marriages and communities of faith in "only God" ways.
+ A couple desires I've had for many years is for married couples to return to God's creational marriage principles of Paradise. And for church leaders to invest the time, energy, and resources in training and equipping their leaders and members in God's creational—mutual equality and functional authority—marriage design.
+ Another long-time desire both Anne and I have prayed about for decades is that God births a Marriage Reformation, and we can be a part of it.

Note: Each of these desires require the involvement of others.

EMOTIONAL MUSCLE MEMORY IN MARRIAGE

In addition to *building* on *goals* and *desires*, we regularly invite couples to develop a tool box full of healthy habits and behaviors. These practices positively imprint on a person and make it easier to advance in intimacy and experience SOUL*gasm* in marriage. So, let's move on as we introduce a few more intimacy-*building* behaviors. This next one is related to *emotional muscle memory*.

If you want to gauge a person's *emotional muscle memory*, all you have to do is observe how they respond in a triggering situation. In other words, what is their knee-jerk response? Often a person's response is an indicator that points toward areas where God wants to heal and restore. Our son-in-law Darren is a good, positive example of this principle. Darren is married to our daughter Cate. Over time, we have observed the way he naturally defaults to presupposing the best in others. His knee-jerk response leans toward being generous and kind, rather than suspicious or judgmental. When a discussion begins to move in a potentially negative direction, he naturally redirects it by responding with kindness and avoiding negativity.

Can we ask, *How about you?* When you are triggered by something, what is your typical response? In marriage, how a spouse responds relates to their experiences. This includes what they saw modeled in their family of origin, the amount of healing they have received, emotional and relational maturity, and the type of *emotional muscle memory* they have developed throughout their lives—and marriage.

Life is lived in a story

anne

One of the highlights of my childhood summers, growing up in a Chicago, suburban bedroom community, was the Fourth of July. I wish I could say it was my patriotism that inspired my Independence Day celebration. But I'm pretty sure I just wanted to submerge myself in all the holiday festivities that our hometown offered.

The official gathering place for Fourth of July was the open field near the center of town. This piece of land included the high school, community pool, Lutheran church, Catholic church and school, and ball fields. There was plenty of room for families to park, party, and picnic. And when the calendar flipped to July, the parade of trucks pulling long trailers signaled the carnival was coming to town!

The majority of carnival booths displayed stuffed animals in every imaginable size and color. Each one represented a reward to the winners. However, the only booth I ever wanted to camp out at was the shooting galleries. Don't ask me why, because no one in my family was a gun activist or liked to hunt. So, I'm not sure where I got my love for shooting at targets.

After we got married, Tim bought me a pellet rifle for my birthday. When I opened my present, I couldn't wait to go into the backyard and shoot at empty cans. Fast forward to a few years ago, a group of women invited me to join them at the local shooting range to get their concealed-weapons carry licenses. I had so much fun. It felt as though something inside of me was waking up from a long slumber.

After I got my concealed carry license, I decided to become a member at a nearby gun club so I could take more classes and have a place where I could shoot. At my first class, the instructor asked us to take out the gun we brought with us. I had a pink camo Walther P22 semi-automatic. Little did I know that gun would be the beginning of a small collection. As a side note, over the years, my son, Tim Jr., has become an expert marksman. Going to the range with him has become a great mom/son bonding time. He continues to challenge me to try something new. So, I've added two more semi-automatics—a Sig Sauer 225 and 238—and two Smith & Wesson revolvers—a 22 and 357—to my collection.

Back to class, the teacher told us how she became a gun safety instructor. Part of her story came from a desire to protect herself after an altercation that she was unprepared for. She shared some stats and told us about a person's fight or flight responses when under stress. And she kept reinforcing the importance of being comfortable with your weapon. As she taught, she referred to a person's initial response as their *muscle memory*. In other words, your initial response to something is much like an involuntary, knee-jerk, reflex reaction. Your body responds to what your muscle remembers. This response is something you learn to control—especially in an emergency situation that includes a deadly weapon.

I'm not sure where the term *muscle memory* came from. I don't believe my muscles have a memory, because my mind controls my muscles. But every woman in the class got her point. The muscle memory phenomenon she kept referring to occurs when a person trains their body, through repetition, how to do something. And this creates a physiological blueprint—a *muscle memory*.

Life is full of stressful situations that offer a short window of time for you to respond. You might be under stress in a self-defense situation that includes a deadly weapon, or maybe you find yourself in a stressful emotional situation in marriage that includes another deadly weapon—your tongue. The Bible says, "The tongue is a deadly arrow."[14] Both a firearm and a person's tongue can be dangerous, and if you are not prepared to handle them correctly, either can result in hurting yourself and others.

Can you see how the muscle memory I learned in my firearm's course can relate to developing emotional muscle memory in marriage? For example, when your spouse disrespects or insults you, what is your emotional muscle memory? Or if your spouse triggers you in some way, what is your knee-jerk reaction? Couples respond in both positive and negative ways, depending on their muscle memory.

Training is a practice. Every time I practice being loving and kind, and responding calmly, I *build* my emotional muscle memory in positive ways. That discipline, or training, prepares me for the moments in life when I am triggered. In those moments, I want my knee-jerk response to be life-giving—not destructive.

ARE YOU UP FOR A REAL LIFE CHALLENGE?

Begin by evaluating your emotional muscle memory, then go on a date with your spouse and ask for their perspective. Celebrate the positive ways you emotionally respond to each other. And review any negative ways you respond to each other. Then, agree to focus on developing two new ways you can increase your emotional muscle memory in kind and life-giving ways. After implementing these, let's say for three months, go on another date and process how your kind and life-giving emotional muscle memory has impacted your intimacy and SOUL*gasm* experiences.

As we conclude this chapter, we pray readers are encouraged to *love* and *respect* each other. This does not happen magically. It is the result of a series of choices a person makes to grow and mature, both individually and together as one. As we move on, we will continue to suggest practical ways to live in the Larger Story, which will lead to celebrating *ordinary* and *extraordinary* moments—and experiencing SOUL*gasm*.

CHAPTER 6

ENJOYING STEPS OF INTIMACY

The word *intimacy* includes emotional, physical, and sexual aspects. Advancing in intimacy is not only satisfying, it is progressive. Marital intimacy—knowing and being more fully known—helps couples to better understand what it means to be "naked without shame"[1]; and enables them to experience SOUL*gasm*. Order and steps remind a person that advancing in intimacy is a process.[2] Of course, people experience varying levels of intimacy with a variety of people, depending on the type of relationship they share. However, our position is that the later steps of intimacy in the following list are reserved for interactions between a husband and wife.

1- Eye to body

Imagine walking into a room full of people with an expectation of meeting someone new. The first thing you might do is take a visual overview of the room. As your eyes scan the crowd, you are able to gather quite a bit of data without ever saying a word. Eye-to-body contact has the power to carry a clear message. There is a distinguishable difference between a friendly nonsexual glance, an admiring gaze, a judging stare, and inappropriate sexual stare. The data provided by eye-to-body contact determines how you will proceed with the next step.

2- Eye to eye

Once a person experiences connection with another person through eye-to-body contact, they may advance to eye-to-eye contact. We have all heard the expression, "The eyes are the window to the soul." Looking into a person's eyes requires an increased level of intimacy. In marriage, eye contact can be a way to advance in intimacy. For example, at Billy Graham's memorial service, his son Franklin told a story about his mom being on bedrest at the end of her life. His dad would sit by her bedside for hours as they lovingly stared into each other's eyes. Their gaze was so intimate that Franklin wondered if he should step out of the room.

Life is lived in a story

tim

When our kids were young, I remember coming home after a busy shift on duty at the firehouse. I was sitting in my chair, reading the sports section of the newspaper. My daughter Colleen jumped on my lap and said, "Daddy, watch me dance." I was so involved in reading the paper that I simply nodded and mumbled, "Okay, I'm watching. Go ahead." She jumped off my lap and began dancing around the living room.

A few minutes passed, and she realized I was not watching her. So, she made additional attempts to get my attention. When I did not respond as she desired, she strategically worked her way under the newspaper and climbed onto my lap. However, she was still unable to make direct eye contact with me. By this time, I had stopped reading the paper and was enjoying watching her try to get my undivided attention. Sitting directly in front of me, she placed her little hands on each side of my face. With the determination of a four-year-old, she turned my head toward hers to make eye contact. In a firm voice she said, "Daddy, look at me. Will you *pleeease* watch me dance?"

Eye-to-eye contact communicates varying levels of intimacy. Have you ever responded negatively to your spouse after receiving "The Look" from him or her? Have you felt the tenderness of your spouse's affection as he or she gazes romantically into your eyes? A variety of powerful messages can be communicated through eye-to-eye contact.

3- Voice to voice

The next step in advancing in intimacy is actually speaking to the person. This may sound basic, but it affirms the progressive nature of intimacy. These steps of intimacy often become more apparent when specific steps are skipped. For example, have you ever had a conversation with someone who didn't give you eye contact? When the other person is looking over your head, looking past you, continually glancing at their watch, or at other people? It's difficult to experience connection without eye contact.

While Steps 1 through 3 reflect the progressive nature of intimacy, each step represents varying levels of intimacy. They also are in play in different types of relationships. For example, eye-to-body contact can be defined as a nonsexual glance to a friend, or a gaze that is more sexually charged between lovers. Women are quick to discern the difference. When inappropriate steps of intimacy are taken, it can feel like a violation to the other person. Eye-to-eye contact can communicate different levels of love, friendship, and acceptance. Similarly, voice-to-voice contact can communicate a number of different things, depending on whether the tone is friendly, inviting, critical, or sexual.

+ + +

On the continuum of intimacy, steps 4 through 7 signal a deeper level of relationship.

4- Hand to hand

Holding hands with another person can be sexual or nonsexual. Certainly, holding hands with a child is different than holding hands with your lover. However, both involve a deeper step in intimacy. You generally would not hold hands with a stranger or even a casual acquaintance, but you might take the hand of another person while praying together at church, signifying your shared relationship as children of God.

5- Hand to shoulder

Steps of intimacy are progressive. Placing your arm around somebody's shoulder and drawing them in to your side is more intimate than holding someone's hand. For example, a parent's hand around a child's shoulder is very different from a couple who are in love.

6- Hand to waist

Placing your hands around a person's waist is more intimate than holding hands or placing your arm around a person's shoulder. This level of contact generally is enjoyed in encounters between parent and child or between husband and wife.

7- Hand to hair

Often people don't consider their heads an intimate part of their body. But stop and think for a moment: A person would never walk up to someone they just met and touch their hair. Strokes to the hair or head imply tenderness and a deeper level of intimacy. For example, we recently observed our daughter Amy fixing our granddaughter's hair. It was such an intimate mommy/daughter time between them.

Life is lived in a story

anne

When the kids were little, Saturday night was bath night. I found that getting four kids ready for church the next morning in a home with one bathtub required a system. I would fill up the tub, and one by one, I would rotate each of our four kids in and out of the bath. I would dry them off, wrap them in a towel, and send them to their bedrooms to put on their pajamas. Once they were dressed, Tim would help dry and comb each one's hair. It was a sweet and intimate part of our weekend routine.

8- Face to face

This face-to-face step of intimacy refers to kissing. In biblical times, followers of Christ were repeatedly commanded to "greet one another with a holy kiss."[3] Many cultures continue this practice. In our family, and with many of our friends, we often kiss one another on the cheek. In certain cultures, greeting a person with a kiss is being polite.

In 1997 a book titled *I Kissed Dating Goodbye*[4] grew in popularity, as over 800,000 copies were sold. The book's message of waiting until a person was married before they kissed was embraced by many Christians. It became a new model for dating and relationships.

Of course, engaged couples are free to choose their boundaries and whether or not they want to kiss. Personally, we would not fall into the camp that promotes waiting until marriage to kiss a future spouse. When we speak to young adults that lean more toward the conservative side, we are often asked if kissing between unmarried couples is okay. In order to answer that question, we ask a few questions to help them differentiate between the different kinds of kissing. We like to take every opportunity to affirm God's design that men and women are sexual beings.

Then we say that, in our opinion, kissing is not sinful. However, sexual boundaries are important during dating. So, the question for us is not "Is kissing okay?" A better question is "What kind of kissing am I comfortable engaging in that will enable me to maintain my sexual boundaries?" It's important to clarify, What do you mean by kissing? Are you talking about a peck on the cheek, a closed-mouth kiss, an open-mouth kiss, or a French kiss? Are these short kisses or long, passionate kissing sessions? Does the kind of kissing you are engaging in stimulate sexual arousal for one or both partners? Does it stimulate fantasy or lust in one or both partners? Does it stimulate an erection for the man? Does kissing lead to deeper stages of intimacy that make it more difficult to maintain sexual boundaries? These are just some of the clarifying questions that are important to explore.

Some premarital couples may be able to enjoy kissing as an expression of intimacy yet be able to maintain healthy, mutually agreed upon boundaries before marriage. Other couples may struggle for a variety of reasons. For some, kissing is an enjoyable form of intimacy. For others, it may be a temptation that causes them to progress to deeper steps in intimacy. Although statistics indicate the majority of Christians have sex before marriage,[5] we believe it is wise for couples to remain abstinent before marriage. This includes physical/sexual boundaries as well as emotional/heart boundaries. However, this requires the couple to be processing together, and communicating in healthy ways, to develop healthy boundaries that will enable them to successfully maintain purity and honor in themselves, and the person they are dating.

As an aside, married couples often tell us they wish kissing were a bigger part of their sexual intimacy. This step of intimacy often gets shortchanged or even bypassed as a couple is free to move on to steps of advanced intimacy. Therefore, we encourage husbands and wives to communicate their desires to one another, and consider going back to some of the initial steps of intimacy to increase their sexual enjoyment.

+ + +

On the continuum of intimacy, steps 9 through 12 are more advanced steps of intimacy.

9- Hand to body

In marriage, a husband and wife are free to enjoy each other's bodies. The skin serves as the largest erogenous zone on a spouse's body. It is filled with nerve endings that are designed to relax, comfort, and stimulate. Using your hands to gently explore each other's bodies is an advanced form of intimacy that has unlimited potential to communicate nonverbal messages of tenderness, comfort, security, sexual arousal, and delight to your spouse.

10- Mouth to body

Gently exploring your spouse's body with your mouth can also be a deeply satisfying step of intimacy. Mouth-to-body contact can communicate powerful messages of love, joy, and commitment to your spouse.

11- Outercourse

This is a term used to describe various forms of foreplay couples use to stimulate one another to orgasm without penetration. Outercourse is a step of intimacy that invites a couple to learn more about each other's body and discover how your spouse responds to specific forms of touch. Communicating sexual preferences and desires to your spouse is an advanced step in intimacy that requires time and trust.

12- Intercourse

Sexual intercourse is often considered the ultimate step of intimacy. This intimate sexual act becomes a symbol of "two becoming one."[6] However, we believe that a husband and wife "becoming one" includes much more than sexual intercourse. Nonetheless, God designed the male and female body to respond to the progressive stages of intercourse with intensifying phases of excitement that can lead to orgasm. The moment of climax is often described as intense pleasure followed by a sense of deep relaxation.

We've spent time describing twelve steps of intimacy because we believe it is important for men and women to understand intimacy's progressive nature. Recognizing these distinct steps can help a couple in setting boundaries in their relationships outside of marriage; and it provides an opportunity to openly discuss how to incorporate steps in ways they find mutually satisfying.

Our counseling experiences suggest that understanding steps of intimacy in marriage can help a husband and wife celebrate *ordinary* and *extraordinary* moments, and this leads to advancing in intimacy and experiencing more frequent SOUL*gasms*. In the next chapter, we will focus on the latter steps of intimacy, and we will unapologetically declare that *God is pro-sex!*

CHAPTER 7

SOUL*GASM* SEX

Life is lived in a story

anne

A woman who was struggling in her marriage came to see us. She had been married for seven years, and she desperately wanted her marriage to be different than what she was currently experiencing; as well as different from what she observed in her parents' marriage. With a high divorce rate in her family line, she was determined to be proactive in protecting her marriage. Over the years, she regularly prayed for her marriage and reached out for help from pastors and counselors. However, none of her attempts resulted in the marital intimacy she longed for.

We listened as she shared examples of how her spiritual, relational, and emotional connection with her husband was a series of disappointments. We noticed she never mentioned anything about their sexual intimacy. When we asked her to share, "What part does sexual intimacy play in your marriage?" she seemed surprised, almost confused by our question. It was as if she didn't understand how sex could have anything to do with the various struggles she was experiencing.

She responded, saying, "With the exception of our early marriage years, sex has never been what I imagined or hoped it would be. It's just been another area of disappointment. Whenever we do have sex, I feel disconnected; it's like an obligation I have to fulfill, just another thing to check off my to-do list."

We asked her to clarify, "What do you mean when you say, 'whenever we do have sex'? When was the last time you and your husband were sexually intimate?"

She paused and said, "It's been over a year."

Whenever clients make the decision to discontinue sex, we explore that with them by asking them to help us understand how they arrived at that decision. In this case, the woman replied, "At that time we were seeing a Christian counselor who told us, 'Sex is not a foundational part of marriage.' The counselor suggested we should focus more on our spiritual and emotional intimacy."

Whenever we talk to clients or lead *NAKED* (*Reclaiming Sexual Intimacy in Marriage*) marriage gatherings, we begin by declaring that *God is pro-sex!* Why do we emphasize that God is pro-sex? Because sex is God's idea, and we believe that sexual intimacy is a foundational part of every marriage relationship. Therefore, it's never a surprise to us when the Enemy targets a couple's sexual intimacy. His attacks include introducing confusion, shame, disappointment, and misunderstanding into a couple's sexual relationship. The Enemy understands the benefits—and protection—for couples who invest in a healthy sex life.

We want to encourage readers; the truth is our personal and professional experience has shown us that *every* married couple struggles with sexual intimacy to one degree or another. Sexual intimacy in marriage is much more than having intercourse and experiencing orgasms. Those can be accomplished without the emotional and spiritual bonding that God designed for couples. Advancing in emotional and sexual intimacy includes understanding God's purposes for sex, processing through your sexual histories, exploring family-of-origin issues, and enjoying all the steps of intimacy. And this opens the door for couples to celebrate *ordinary* and *extraordinary* moments, experience SOUL*gasm*, and enjoy a vibrant sex life.

GOD'S PURPOSES FOR SEXUAL INTIMACY

This book's primary focus is emotional intimacy. There are many ways that a person can care for their soul and the soul of their marriage; one of them is through sexual intimacy. However, it's important for husbands and wives to be reminded that when they grow in experiencing a deep soul connection with their spouse, it leads them through the steps of intimacy, and creates an increased desire for sexual connection. Without a healthy soul connection, sex can become a disconnected activity that offers limited satisfaction. Disconnected sex falls way short of God's desire to increase a couple's bond and celebrate being "naked without shame."

Pause for a moment and consider your answer to this question, *Why did God create marital sex?* We believe that God designed sex for five primary purposes.[1]

> 1. Marital Sex Is for **Celebration**. The first thing we learn about humankind from the Creation story is that every man and every woman are made in the image

of God.[2] Maleness and masculinity, and femaleness and femininity, are intrinsic parts of every man and woman. One man and one woman are intrinsic parts of God's creational marriage design. God invites every husband and wife to celebrate unity, diversity, community, and mutuality in marriage. These are to be experienced within the permanence and exclusivity of the marriage covenant. Our experience has taught us that couples who are taking steps to live out a healthy sexual relationship have limitless potential to advance in intimacy—in knowing and being fully known.

The Bible says, "Whatever you do in word or deed, *do all* in the name of the Lord Jesus."[3] *All* includes emotional intimacy and sexual intimacy, including orgasm. Therefore, sex is designed to be a celebration—an act of worship. As you re-read the above passage, "Whatever you do in word or deed, do *all* in the name of the Lord Jesus," have you ever thought of sexual intimacy and experiencing SOUL*gasm* in marriage as something you can do *in the name of the Lord Jesus*—as acts of worship? If this is a new concept to you, please remember that we are not worshiping sexual intimacy and SOUL*gasm*; we are worshiping the God who created them.

Marital sex is an invitation for couples to advance in intimacy as they love, serve, and enjoy each other— *together* rejoicing in being "naked without shame." However, far too many husbands and wives have allowed the Enemy to *block* them from experiencing this deep level of connection with God and their spouse. If this describes you, we want to encourage you to explore any issues that *block* you from the sexual celebration God intended for you to enjoy.

2. Another purpose for marital sex is **Procreation**. Beginning with the first married couple, God commanded the husband and wife to reproduce—to "be fruitful and multiply."[4] Every child has immeasurable value because he or she is made in the image of God. In marriage, having children provides opportunities to reproduce—to expand community—and teach children life-giving godly values that are to be passed on to future generations.

   However, it is important to keep in mind that being fruitful and multiplying is not limited to having biological children. It includes adoption, foster parenting, and spiritual parenting. Nevertheless, although fatherhood and motherhood are extremely important, always remember that a person's (married or single) highest calling is to love God with all his or her heart, soul, mind, and strength.[5]

3. Another purpose for marital sex is for **Pleasure**. Despite anything you may have heard to the contrary, God is pro-sex and pro-pleasure. His desire is for married couples to celebrate each other and enjoy a mutually satisfying sex life. Unfortunately, advancing in passion, longing, and in intimacy—in knowing and being fully known—has become somewhat of a lost art in our self-focused "we want it all and we want it now" culture.

   Remember, advancing in marital intimacy—growing in desire and delight—includes a couple experiencing both SOUL*gasm* and orgasm. God created orgasms so a couple could experience deep pleasure emotionally and physically. In marriage, God invites a husband and wife to "*eat ... drink, and imbibe deeply.*"[6]

4. Another purpose for marital sex is **Comfort**. After the death of David and Bathsheba's son, the Bible says, "Then David comforted his wife Bathsheba, and went in to her and lay with her."[7] Life and marriage are difficult. We live in a season of history that includes inordinate amounts of stress, fear, and anxiety. During difficult times in marriage, providing comfort through sexual connection can be a gift from God—through you—to your spouse.

   Instead of viewing pain, loss, and crises as obstacles, couples can view these as opportunities to step into the Larger Story, where God (not self) is the main character, and advance together in love and intimacy. Strengthening marital bonds by serving a spouse emotionally (SOUL*gasm*) and sexually (orgasm) in difficult times, can help to release negative energy, relieve stress, and bring comfort and healing.

5. Another purpose for marital sex is **Protection**. Sexual intimacy creates a strong bond between a husband and wife, a bond that helps protect the marriage relationship. Over the years, we've learned that couples who enjoy a healthy sexual relationship feel more connected spiritually, emotionally, and physically. In addition, they are more joyful and hopeful about their

marriage. The apostle Paul wrote about the sexual relationship of a Christian husband and wife:

"The husband must fulfill his duty to his wife, and likewise also the wife to her husband. The wife does not have authority over her own body, but the husband does; and likewise also the husband does not have authority over his own body, but the wife does. Stop depriving one another, except by agreement for a time, so that you may devote yourselves to prayer, and come together again so that Satan will not tempt you because of your lack of self-control."[8]

"SEXUAL DUTY"

Note to readers: We covered sexual duty in *NAKED*, but it's important enough that we want to revisit it here in SOUL*gasm*.

Life is lived in a story

anne

Whenever we are counseling couples, or leading workshops on sexuality, the 1 Corinthians chapter 7 topic of "sexual duty" always sparks interesting discussions and questions. Often, someone will make a comment in response to the word *duty*. It may sound something like this, "I'm confused, isn't the emotional and sexual intimacy that God designed for marriage supposed to be defined by romance rather than duty?"

For many reasons, the word *duty* seems to be a trigger for some people. To make matters worse, we also teach this passage as a *command to obey*. The word *command* is another word that is often not received well by both wives and husbands. Before we begin to unpack the verse, we read aloud the dictionary definition of *duty* as "a moral or legal obligation; a responsibility."[9] So, before we lose you, let's take a closer look at romance, and how a spouse taking ownership and responsibility to fulfill a sexual duty fits into the discussion.

Life is lived in a story

tim

When I was a firefighter, I worked a twenty-four-hour shift every third day. Reporting for duty meant I was required to be at the firehouse and ready to engage. I loved being a fireman—and many on-duty days were filled with lights and sirens, excitement and risks. But there were plenty of days when I did not feel like reporting for duty. I was exhausted from working seventy-plus hours a week at two different jobs, and often things were stressful at home. On those days, reporting for duty seemed more like *work* than *joy*.

Likewise, there are times in every marriage when sex is an exciting, lights-and-sirens experience. But there are also times when one spouse, or both, are working long hours, and for any number of reasons, they are tired, stressed, and often feel exhausted. During these times, one spouse may desire sexual intimacy and to experience an orgasm and the other spouse does not. On those days, for some couples, sex can feel more like reporting for duty than a celebration of sexual intimacy.

Therefore, having a sense of humor is important in marriage, especially when it comes to sex. For example, I remember early in our marriage when we were first challenged with this teaching, I had never heard anyone discuss sex from the perspective of the word *duty*. Not long after,

I approached my bride, stood at attention, offered a smart salute and declared, "Reporting for duty!" I've found that it's not so much the words I say, it's more about the intention of my heart and the atmosphere I'm trying to create. Anne and I encourage couples to develop their own creative sexual language. For example, one couple we know incorporates playful terms to communicate sexually with one another. When the wife asks her husband, "Is the store open tonight?"—she is *not* talking about the grocery store!

Over the years, we've heard some interesting interpretations of 1 Corinthians 7. For example, we've heard both husbands and wives say, "The Bible says my spouse's body belongs to me. Therefore, my spouse needs to meet my sexual needs!" Clearly, the heart of this passage is not suggesting that by enforcing the law, a couple will be positively motivated to obey.

When a spouse attempts to get their sexual needs met by using shame, guilt, or trying to manipulate a Bible passage, it *blocks* intimacy and damages the relationship. Whenever a spouse defaults to demands, declarations, and control, they miss out on intimately connecting with their spouse. And they forfeit the opportunity for soul connection, which could have led to experiencing SOUL*gasm*.

The heart of this command is for couples to focus on reciprocal servanthood. This is walked out in love, rather than defaulting to selfish control or declaring perceived personal rights. This passage reframes a couple's primary focus away from self, and onto God and His plan for emotional and sexual intimacy. Practically speaking, this includes arranging your priorities so that you are first pleasing God, then loving and serving your spouse, and then having your individual needs met.

The above Bible passage gives only one exception to the command for a husband and wife to fulfill their sexual duty to each other. If a husband and wife decide not to have sex, their decision should meet these criteria: (1) except by agreement (mutual consent); (2) for a time (temporary); (3) to devote themselves to prayer. In other words, a literal interpretation of this passage says the only reason for a husband or wife to withhold sex from each other is when they both agree, for a specific period of time, and for the purpose of prayer.

WHAT IF I DON'T FEEL LIKE FULFILLING MY SEXUAL DUTY?

As an adult, there are plenty of things a person engages in everyday that they don't *feel* like doing. Have you ever *felt* like not going to work, caring for your family, or maintaining your home? Since God created humankind with emotions, *feelings* influence a person's decisions and behavior—but they shouldn't determine the outcome. When it comes to sex, always being "ready, willing, and able" to sexually engage with your spouse is the *ideal* not the norm. Remember, every couple faces stressors, including personal medical concerns, emotional issues, children's needs, work stress, financial problems, issues surrounding pregnancy, anxiety, and depression—just to name a few. And others face even more challenging issues. So, the expectation that a person should always be "ready, willing and available" to engage in sex may be the *ideal*, but it's not the norm because *life happens!*

One important point we hope every reader understands is that this First Corinthians passage is God's *ideal* for husbands and wives to walk out sexual intimacy. Similar to the Great Commandment, which commands Christ-followers to "love God with all your heart, soul, mind, and strength … and to love others as you love yourself"[10]—this is God's *ideal* for love. But for a variety of reasons, the command to love 24 hours a day/365 days a year with all your heart, soul, mind, and strength is next to impossible to walk out. Likewise, for a spouse to be available and eager to engage in sexual intimacy 24 hours a day/365 days a year is next to impossible to walk out.

Whenever couples find themselves on different pages in regard to sexual intimacy, it can create an opportunity to practice love, grace, and forgiveness. We encourage the spouse who, for whatever reasonable reason, does not want to engage in sexual intimacy to be honest about why they'd prefer not to have sex, and share it with their spouse. An honest conversation from the heart can be a moment of bonding rather than communicating rejection. For example, what if the spouse who does not want to have sex agrees to be the one who initiates sex the next time? However, if avoiding sex, or refusing to engage in a healthy conversation, becomes an ongoing problem, we encourage them to seek counsel.

Life is lived in a story, and a person's story includes life experiences that impact their sexuality. Sadly, far too many people have been sinned against, and exposed to some level of abuse. This often leaves them struggling with trust issues that can surface in their marriage. It's not surprising to hear them say, "My body belongs to me, not to my spouse. I would never totally trust my spouse with my body. I want to be able to decide when my body can be enjoyed—after all it's my body."

Submitting sexually is an act of trust. Every person is invited to trust God as they take steps to advance in trusting their spouse. When a person's trust has been violated, it can result in them feeling guarded because it can stir up unresolved pain related to their past. This can include unforgiveness, negative sexual imprinting, as well as any history of abuse. We believe God invites men and women to explore deeper levels of healing in response to potential *blocks* that arise in a person's sexual relationship. These *blocks* can symbolize a yellow flag that God is waving as He invites you to surrender to Him, surrender your pain, and receive His healing. Sexual healing allows a person to enjoy greater freedom and deeper intimacy. Regardless of what a person's story is, we encourage you to always begin by inviting God into the process—**I.O.T.L.** Talk to Him about any hurt, confusion, resistance, control, or rebellion. Again, if processing with the Lord and trusted others does not bring the breakthrough you long for, we encourage you to process your story with a trained Christian counselor who specializes in sexual trauma and abuse.

God designed sex to be an act of worship[11]; it can also be an act of warfare.[12] We find it interesting that at the end of this passage, the apostle Paul wrote that couples who do not deprive one another and fulfill their sexual duty will avoid Satan's temptation.[13] The reality is that there is a spiritual component in sexual intimacy. And apparently Satan understands the power of the sexual dimension of a couple's lives.

We encourage a husband and wife not to view sexual duty as a shame-loaded millstone placed around a spouse's neck. Instead, it can become an invitation to connect with a spouse, live out grace at a deep level, and protect marital oneness. As we re-read this one-of-a-kind command, we wonder: *Might one of God's purposes in giving such a strict command about sexual intimacy be that it invites couples to process and work through any chaos, unforgiveness, or necessary healing that a command of this proportion can stir up?*

OBSTACLE OR OPPORTUNITY?

Loving and serving a spouse by fulfilling a sexual duty can be viewed as an *obstacle* or an *opportunity*. An opportunity to live in the Larger Story where God is the main character (and *it's not about me*), instead of living in the smaller story where "I" am the main character (and *it's all about me*). After decades of living this out in our own marriage, we encourage couples to look for opportunities to serve their spouse sexually, instead of holding on to negative perceptions surrounding sexual duty. Sexual duty is an important part of a marriage covenant. It includes a commitment, as co-leaders and reciprocal servants, to choose to love, serve, and bring pleasure and comfort to a spouse. Our experience has shown us that a spouse's motive, heart, and attitude are keys to fulfilling sexual duty.

God designed sex in marriage for **Celebration + Procreation + Pleasure + Comfort + Protection**. And He invites couples to live out the worship and warfare components in SOUL*gasm* and sexual intimacy. All of these are to be walked out in love and honor: "Let marriage be held in honor among all, and let the marriage bed be undefiled."[14] *Honor* includes "personal integrity; respect; dignity."[15] *Defiled* means "to make something dirty or polluted."[16]

+ + +

#METOO

In recent years, the idea of adding the following in a marriage book would have seemed absurd. But as Bob Dylan the prophetic-poet-singer-songwriter wrote, "For the times they are a-changin'."[17] Our culture is witnessing an ever-increasing amount of sexual abuse accusations toward athletes, coaches, teachers, religious/church leaders, famous entertainers, pundits, politicians, military officers, Hollywood elites, and world-renowned comedians. As this has occurred, new hashtags have emerged; a popular one is called #MeToo.

Sexual abuse—all abuse—negatively impacts advancing in intimacy and experiencing SOULgasm in untold ways. In our REAL LIFE office, a sign hangs on the wall, it reads, "YOUR STORY MATTERS." #MeToo is giving women (and men) an opportunity to share their stories related to sexual assault, abuse, misogyny, and male control. Sadly, the overwhelming majority of people who are sharing heart-wrenching experiences are women. Thankfully, abuses are being exposed, and secrets are being disclosed that have been hidden, denied, suppressed, or repressed.

Our hope is God uses people's stories to help them realize that what happened to them—living with shame, loss of innocence, a fractured heart, wounds to their spirit, body, and soul—was a violation of their personhood, and was not their fault. Our prayer is that every abuse survivor can download into the core of their being that they are a woman (or man) made in God's image—and they matter to God! In addition to giving people an opportunity to have their voices heard, #MeToo highlights the courage, strength, and resiliency of women (and men).

Before moving on, as a husband, wife, pastoral counselors, and ordained ministers, we believe it is important to pause and say to every abuse survivor, "What happened to you was a sin; we are truly sorry; we commend you for your strength and bravery."

WHEN DID MEN ABUSING WOMEN BEGIN?

Our hearts break as we read tragic #MeToo stories. But it makes us wonder: *When did centuries of women being abused by men originate?*

Misogyny (hatred of women), male rulership, hierarchy, and forced female subordination began after sin entered the story.[18] Review the biblical account of creation. *In the beginning,* God created every human—male and female—in His triune image.[19] And God designed full functional equality—intrinsically and functionally—for both the man and woman. Review the text, the man and woman were *both* given the procreation and dominion mandates.[20]

In the beginning, God commanded the man and woman to "become one."[21] Together as "one," the husband and wife celebrated being "naked without shame."[22] Tragically, after sin entered the story, different marriage views were spawned. These included male rulership, hierarchical, and complementarian marriage views. We believe the seeds in these spawned marriage views birthed a culture of male domination, male privilege, along with abusive treatment toward women.

Supporters of marriage views that emerged after the fall—male rulership, hierarchical, complementarian—believe the husband is the wife's "leader" and "spiritual cover." Thankfully, our real-life experience is that traditional/hierarchical/complementarian men are beginning to talk about their leadership and perceived authority in more egalitarian ways. Our prayer is that their words morph into actions that include treating women as "co-leaders, co-servants, and co-equals in Christ."[23] Unfortunately, many religious leaders do not base their marriage teachings on God's creational design. And this results in perspectives that include the husband being God's designated leader and "spiritual cover."

If you believe in a hierarchical marriage view, review the Bible. It commands *mutual submission* to every follower of Christ: "Be subject to one another in the fear of Christ."[24] Regarding authority, a passage that men who push back against full functional equality tend to avoid is 1 Corinthians 7:4, which clearly commands *mutual authority* between a husband and wife.

As far as the husband being the wife's "spiritual cover," 1 Timothy 2:5 (NIV) says, "For there is one God and one mediator between God and [human] kind, the man Jesus Christ." Our take is that women and men—wives and husbands—are to go directly to Jesus Christ; they are not to go first through any person—spouse, saint, or religious leader.

Looking back throughout history, we see abuse and mistreatment of women as fruit from the seeds of sin that was rooted in the fall. Which makes us wonder: *Might men who insist on having authority and being the leader and "spiritual cover," be missing out on the power, protection, and kingdom-advancing potential in living out functional equality? And what if women returned to the full functional equality and mutuality principles of Paradise, as they passionately exercised all the gifts God has given them—without restrictions?*

Throughout the Bible, Christ-followers are exhorted to focus on what *builds up the church.*[25] We believe as courageous men push back against tradition, culture, religiosity, shame, fear, and control, they will realize the benefits in full functional equality. And the good news is when religious leaders stop restricting women—who make up over half of their communities of faith—from utilizing *all* the gifts God has given them, this will *build up the church* and advance God's kingdom.

Life is lived in a story

tim

I think this is a good place to pause and specifically address men. A main focus in this book is on SOUL*gasm* in marriage. And we offer a number of SOUL*gasm builders* and *blockers*. However, one key component that Anne and I believe is crucial to experiencing SOUL*gasm* in marriage directly relates to a husband-wife-couple's marriage view. Our position is that traditional/ hierarchical/ complementarian marriage views inhibit a husband-wife-couple from advancing in intimacy, celebrating SOUL*gasm*, and maximizing kingdom of God potential when compared to God's creational marriage design.

If you are a man, I'd like to ask you a few important questions:

Are you willing to fully embrace full functional equality?

Are you willing to destroy your male trump card?

Are you willing to reject male privileges?

Are you willing to become a champion for women to be treated as functional equals?

Are you willing to do everything you can to help women to use ALL the gifts God has given them without any restrictions?

To utilize a fire department term, will you be a "first responder" when you observe any man discounting, devaluing, mocking, or mistreating a woman?

Men, as a retired fire chief, will you permit me to use some firehouse slang? In the fire service, when a firefighter did something extraordinary—when they clearly stood out "above the rest"—we respectfully referred to them—both men and women—(figuratively speaking) as "having balls as big as boxcars!"

If it were possible, to every man who is willing to passionately live out the above equality, mutuality, and co-leadership challenges, I would look you directly in the eyes and say, *"You have balls as big as boxcars!"* Seriously, Anne and I believe with all our hearts that as men truly value women as full functional equals, this will become a church and relationship game-changer. And it will help to turn the tide related to the devaluing and abuse of women. Instead of adding more #MeToo stories, we envision a new hashtag emerging possibly called #CoLeader-CoServant-CoEqual-in-Christ that will describe stories about full functional equality—without any restrictions—and how it is impacting lives, building up the church, and advancing God's kingdom.

Our prayer is that more and more church/ministry leaders will stand before their staff, congregation, and teams. They will humbly say to women, "We are truly sorry for any ways that you have been disrespected, discounted, and restricted from using *all* the gifts God has given you." Leaders will recognize the damage that's been done to God's original design for women. Their words will include action-steps as they become champions for women. *Now that would be an epic, boxcar statement!*

+ + +

GOD IS PRO-SEX

Before moving on to the next chapter, as we've previously stated, sexual intimacy impacts every married couple. In this chapter, we've highlighted a handful of important issues concerning intimacy and sexuality. For any reader who wants additional information, we cover many topics in our *NAKED: Reclaiming Sexual intimacy in Marriage* book set. The topics include emotional and sexual intimacy, understanding the importance of sexual imprinting and sexual histories, breaking soul ties, pushing back against the devastating effects of pornography, sexual agreement, and a number of sensitive, sexual issues that a person rarely, if ever, hears addressed in churches.[26]

Oneness in marriage is multi-faceted: SPIRIT oneness includes under-standing your true identity—that you are a *beloved* daughter or son of a good God. Spiritual nakedness involves **I.O.T.L.** and including God in everything. SOUL oneness includes emotional nakedness (SOUL*gasm*) and involves a spouse, figuratively speaking, removing emotional fig leaves from their heart, mind, and soul. This becomes the pathway for couples to celebrate BODY oneness that includes celebrating physical nakedness, sexual intimacy, SOUL*gasm*, and orgasm. All that is to say, we'd like to conclude this chapter by again saying—*God is pro-sex!*

PART TWO
SOUL*gasm* BLOCKERS

"One of the hardest things in life to learn are which bridges to cross and which bridges to burn."

Oprah Winfrey

+ + +

In Part One, SOUL*gasm* BUILDERS, we included a number of principles that *build* intimacy in marriage. These principles focus on the influence of your family of origin, celebrating your spouse's uniqueness, roles and functions, love and respect, steps of intimacy, and SOUL*gasm* sex. They challenged couples to advance in intimacy, positioning them to celebrate life's *ordinary* and *extraordinary* moments, and experience SOUL*gasm*.

In Part Two, SOUL*gasm* BLOCKERS, we will address a number of things that *block* a couple from advancing in intimacy. When a person is able to identify negative patterns in their life, it gives them the opportunity to make different choices. As a side note, we strongly encourage couples to invest in going through the SOUL*gasm Companion Journal* that dovetails with this book. It provides questions and applications to every chapter. It can be completed as a couple, or in a small group.

CHAPTER 8

SOWING AND REAPING

When you hear the word *law*, what do you think of? Our lives are influenced by all different kinds of laws, including legal laws, such as exceeding the speed limit, driving while intoxicated, and meeting building construction requirements. There are also moral laws. For example, the Ten Commandments include prohibitions against committing murder, adultery, lying, and stealing. There are natural laws, such as the law of gravity, motion, and aerodynamics. However, it's easy to overlook the power of spiritual laws that are found throughout the New Testament. The ones we've included in this section are *sowing and reaping, judging, handling offenses, honoring parents*, and *pride and humility*. Sometimes these laws can overlap. For example, sowing and reaping often relates to judging.

Spiritual laws have potential to set both positive and negative things in motion. When husbands and wives choose to make godly choices regarding how they respond to one another, they begin to experience the blessings related to obedience. Their intimacy level deepens as they position themselves to experience SOUL*gasm* moments.

Sowing and reaping is a biblical term that is rarely used in our culture, or in conversational ways. However, it is a spiritual law that will never become outdated. The principles it highlights will help every couple advance in intimacy with God, their spouse, and others. So, let's begin to unpack how this spiritual law impacts your life and marriage.

The Bible says, "Do not be deceived, God is not mocked; for whatever a man sows, this he will also reap."[1] A familiar firehouse version of this passage is "What goes around comes around." In other words, there is a spiritual law called the law of *sowing and reaping* that sets positive or negative things in motion and impacts many areas in a person's life and marriage. This law also includes a multiplication principle. Second Corinthians 9:6 reads, "He who sows sparingly will also reap sparingly, and he who sows bountifully will also reap bountifully." For example, a person sows (plants) seeds; and when they are nurtured in good soil, the seeds produce exponentially more than the initial seeds that were planted.

Think about your family of origin, what kinds of seeds—both positive and negative—did your family sow and reap? For example, have you observed any specific positive or negative character traits and behaviors in your family line? Do you ever notice that these same traits and behaviors are being reproduced in your own life, or in the lives of your children and grandchildren? Do you find yourself doing things your parents did that you swore you would never do? This may be an indication that the law of sowing and reaping is in play.

Now consider your marriage, what kinds of seeds do you sow, and what does your spouse sow? Can we ask, *What are you, your spouse, and your marriage reaping?* For example, do you sow seeds of unconditional love, kindness, grace, joy, and forgiveness? Or do you sow seeds of shame, blame, fear, control, anger, comparison, jealousy, and competition?

Life is lived in a story

tim

In my early twenties, I justified the ways I judged church leadership by referring to it as *critiquing*. I considered it to be the same way the fire department critiqued every fire or emergency incident. Truth be told, I thought my critiquing was part of my leadership gift! Some of my critiquing included, "I just didn't connect to the pastor's illustration today. Why couldn't he have used a more realistic example?" Or I would listen as a passage was preached, and focus on the points I thought the teacher missed.

On occasion I would say to Anne, "I work seventy-plus hours per week. What do pastors have to do besides pray, attend meetings, and prepare a thirty-minute message? It must be nice to just work on Sundays."

But *what goes around comes around*. And after working twenty-plus years on the fire department, I took an early retirement and went to work full time on a church staff. And guess what occurred? After sowing critical comments and judgment toward my church leaders, as a new church leader, my precious sheep began "critiquing" me! I would hear comments, such as *Tim can be so abrasive; Tim may know a lot about fighting fires— but he's a little light on the Word!*

Now that I was a full-time, paid pastor—a man of the cloth—I was being judged and getting sheep-bites all the time. *Why?* Because "Whatever a man sows, this he will also reap."[2] I had sown critical comments and judgment, and I was reaping critical comments and judgment.

The law of sowing and reaping has both negative and positive fruit in marriages, families, and relationships. To offer an example of negative fruit in marriage, we recall counseling a couple where the husband was extremely critical and unkind to his wife. It seemed at every crossroad, he would sow negative and critical words toward her. To him, his wife just never seemed to be enough. From his perspective, she didn't dress the way he wanted, and she didn't put on her makeup or fix her hair the way he wanted. He was critical about her family and friendships, her cooking, how she managed the home, parented the kids, and how she engaged in physical/sexual intimacy. As counselors, we considered this husband's control, negativity, and critical comments toward his wife as both active and passive abusive behavior. His marriage seemed to consist of a never-ending list of *shoulds*. Of course, his *shoulds* were always according to *his* version of life.

At one session, I asked the husband if he thought the way he treated his wife was in line with biblical principles for marriage. He replied, "Look, I am a successful business leader in the community and an elder at my church. My wife's responsibilities include a few simple things: She is to focus on submitting to me, serving me, and meeting my sexual needs."

As the man continued to sow misogynistic behaviors that included hyper-control and criticalness into his marriage—guess what he reaped? Besides his marriage being in a constant state of chaos, lacking intimacy, and SOUL*gasm* nowhere on the radar, his family was a mess. His wife became so hurt, angry, and disconnected from him that she ended up committing adultery with a casual friend who encouraged her and treated her with kindness.

Thankfully, the husband was willing to take responsibility for how damaging his style of relating was. And his wife was willing to look at how her passivity contributed to the breakdown of their marriage. They entered a season of counseling, dedicated to their own inner healing. Over time, their marriage didn't just survive, it actually began to thrive. This became evident as the husband and wife sowed love, forgiveness, and kindness into their hearts, lives, and marriage, and then reaped those things individually—and as a couple.

We recall counseling another couple who both came from divorced homes. From their premarital days, they were committed to doing whatever it took to have not just a *good* marriage—they wanted to experience God's creational "two become one" and "naked and not ashamed" description of marriage.[3] They were both hungry to learn more about marriage and were very teachable. They joined a small group that included a few other couples with strong marriages. Over time, as they became friends with others in the group, they were able to observe more experienced married couples lead by example. God was inviting this couple to grow and mature through the support of their community. It changed the way they viewed their marriage as they began looking for ways to love, serve, and be kind to each other. Being around other godly couples allowed them to observe the loving and respectful ways other couples treated each other.

Once again, the sowing and reaping principle began to bear fruit. Their intimacy and oneness kept increasing to deeper levels. Over the years, as they continued to sow positive lifegiving words and behaviors, they experienced a marriage that was very different from either one of their families. This couple began to regularly experience SOUL*gasm* moments that turned the *ordinary* into the *extraordinary*. Five years later, they led their own couples small group. They had become a model for younger couples. Their marriage became an example that others wanted to emulate. And this opened doors to share about God—the Maker of marriage.

We realize the above negative and positive marriage examples are more extreme in nature. However, in counseling sessions, we can often identify couples who are advancing in intimacy, oneness, and SOUL*gasm* by the seeds they sow into each other.

HOW ABOUT YOU?

The Bible says, "Pay close attention to yourself and to your teaching."[4] Can we ask you a few questions?

+ Do you regularly default to being critical?
+ Do you see yourself as a person who routinely unrighteously judges others?
+ Are you quick to look for the "speck" in another person's eye, rather than consider the possibility of a "log" in your own eyes?[5]
+ Do you have a lot of opinions about the way things "should" be? (Of course, *should* is according to *you*.)
+ Do you have a lot to say about decisions your spouse and other people make?
+ Do you come from a family of people who sow negativity into relationships?
+ Do you behave like some religious-leaning folks who quickly go stealth, and put a toxic-religious spin on their control and narcissistic self-assurance that *their* way is always the *right* way?

If you relate to any of the above negative behaviors, we challenge you to consider seeking godly counsel, and invest in inner healing. Also, take note of the community that surrounds you. Do you have friends who model strong marriages? Who are the godly examples in your life? Remember, God can turn marriage *obstacles* into *opportunities*—opportunities to experience *ordinary* and *extraordinary* moments, advance in intimacy, and experience SOUL*gasm*—if you let Him.

Life is lived in a story

tim

I regularly meet with a good friend, "Ed," who has been married more than twenty years. He has kids in high school and college; and one of the desires of his heart is not to be just a *good* husband and dad, but to be the *best* husband and dad he can be. We were recently at lunch, and after catching up on life, he asked, "Tim, how are you doing in your marriage?" I always appreciate that question because although Anne and I ask that question regularly in our counseling office, I hardly ever get asked that question.

I paused and thought to myself, *Hmm, how am I doing in our marriage?* At first, my mind went to a file of beliefs and behaviors. But then, I took a deep breath and did a quick heart check. I paused to inquire of the Lord (**I.O.T.L.**) and focused on *listening* to the Holy Spirit. Looking directly into my friend's eyes, I said, "Ed, that might be a question you'd like to ask Anne. But since you're asking me, I guess I can say, in all humility, I believe I am doing pretty good as a husband. But here's my disclaimer: Of course, I still have a lot to learn about this thing called 'marital-oneness.' Plus, I've lived long enough to know that where a person feels the *least* vulnerable, can be the place they are *most* vulnerable. That's just one reason why I try never to take my marriage for granted. Anne and I sure don't have all the answers. In fact, sometimes we don't even know the right questions to ask. But after forty-plus years, we understand this, 'Those who marry will have troubles.'"[6]

I continued, "No one ever arrives in marriage—it's a journey. For Anne and me, there are always going to be areas where we disagree or get triggered. But to answer your question, *How am I doing in our marriage?* I say this humbly—and if Anne were here, I think she would agree—that this is one of the best seasons in our married life."

Ed said, "That's so good to hear, Tim. I wish I heard it more often." Wanting me to unpack that a bit more, Ed asked, "So, tell me more about *how* you are being the husband you desire to be?"

Again, I paused and then replied, "I believe after more than forty-one years of marriage, I am more purposefully focusing on God. I was always a person who could quickly default to completing my daily to-do list, but as I get older, I am treasuring just being with God. And as far as my marriage, I regularly ask the Holy Spirit to help me love Anne unconditionally, and this includes being kind to her."

Ed gave me a quizzical look and said, "Okay, but what exactly does that look like?"

I replied, "I ask the Lord to help me see Anne in the amazing ways that He sees her."

"Tim, that sounds so hyper-spiritual. Give me a real-life example of what being a good husband who is kind to Anne looks like?"

"Okay, here's a simple example. Yesterday morning I was up early. I like to get into the office to write before our counseling schedule kicks in. I always start my day with God. I want Him to lead my day so I **I.O.T.L.** and invite Him to tell me anything He wants to tell me. So, as I'm walking out the back door, I glance downstairs and see a pile of laundry on the floor. First off, Anne and I both participate in managing and maintaining our home. That includes doing laundry, cleaning, cooking, household upkeep, and so on. But when I saw the laundry, I knew she would do it before heading to the office. I also know Anne's number one love language is service. So, whenever I serve Anne, it screams to her heart and soul, 'I love and care about you!'

"In a milli-second, I sensed the Lord inviting me to get that load of laundry started before heading to the office. I had a choice to listen and obey or to dismiss that still, soft voice. So, I set down my stuff and put my immediate plans on hold. I went downstairs, folded the laundry in the dryer, and started a new load."

Ed was listening and nodding as I spoke. He replied, "So, do I have this right, you relate kindness to doing laundry?"

I smiled and said, "Well, yes and no. For me, the piece of gold in this laundry story is taking the time to **I.O.T.L.** and invite God into my process. Yesterday, that resulted in God inviting me to an act of kindness—which happened to be starting a load of laundry.

"Ed, when I was younger, being a good husband who was kind to his wife was often connected to things I could easily do for her. Things that didn't really cost me anything. For example, I could say, 'I love you,' buy her a gift, or give her a foot massage (with the hopes it would lead to having sex). For too many years, I was busy achieving my goals and desires and executing my action plans. I pretty much limited my relationship with God to a Sunday morning service, or to a few minutes every morning. I did that for too many decades, but as I grow older, I understand that relationship with God is an ongoing, moment-by-moment experience that includes invitations to celebrate the *ordinary* and *extraordinary* moments. For me, as I did laundry, an *ordinary* moment became an *extraordinary* moment because it included God—and blessed my bride.

"Ed, how about you? *How are you being a good husband?*"

Ed squirmed in his seat and said, "I rarely, if ever, invite God into my marriage—yet alone day-to-day moments. And as I think about your simple laundry example, I have to admit that my kindness is usually programmed."

"Programmed in what ways?" I asked.

"My kindness typically involves things that I like and are easy for me to do. For example, I'll pick up dinner on the way home from work, or suggest we go on a movie date–of course, to see a movie I want to see. I can take the kids to a sporting event I'm interested in, buy my wife chocolate, or initiate sex. But I guess when I soberly review my 'kindness' ... bottom line, it's pretty much *all about me.*"

I replied, "Ed, it's never too late to include God, invite Him to help you make changes, and focus on becoming more loving and kind. And when you do that, the spiritual law of sowing and reaping kicks in. Going back to your initial question, *how am I doing in my marriage?* I believe including God and responding to the Holy Spirit's leading—those are the major reasons why I think that Anne and I are in our best season of our marriage."

The spiritual law of sowing and reaping is in play, whether a person recognizes it—or believes it. You can refer to it as, "What goes around comes around." But in life and marriage, sowing criticism and negativity will become a SOUL*gasm blocker*. And sowing life-giving words and positivity will become a SOUL*gasm builder*.

CHAPTER 9

UNRIGHTEOUS JUDGING

Have you ever played the Lotto? In 2016, Americans invested over 70 billion dollars in this game of chance.[1] That's a lot of money that unfortunately does not have a very good return on your investment.

In this chapter, we would like to offer you something that we guarantee will provide a great return on your time investment. Let's begin by looking at the Word of God. The Bible says, "He who is spiritual appraises all things ..."[2] But a passage in Matthew chapter 7 seems to say the opposite. It reads, "Do not judge, or you too will be judged. For in the same way you judge others, you will be judged, and with the measure you use, it will be measured to you."[3] Another passage says, "... everyone of you who passes judgment, for in that which you judge another, you condemn yourself."[4] So, which one is right?

We'd like to highlight two kinds of judgment, righteous and unrighteous. First, righteous judgment includes evaluating circumstances and making decisions; it's a part of life. We make righteous judgments everyday as responsible adults. For example, *What mechanic should I take my car to? What school is best for my children to attend? Who should I choose as our dentist? What local church should our family invest in? Is this a wise purchase or financial investment to make?*

On the other hand, Matthew 7 says, "Do not judge." Other translations say, "Judge not." This verse is not referring to righteous judgment. It's not the same as *appraising* someone or something as a responsible adult in order to make a godly decision. Matthew 7 refers to condemning someone on moral grounds and passing judgment on them.

THERE ARE MORE THAN TWO SIDES TO EVERY STORY

When we were younger, we tended to believe that every story had two sides—my side and the other person's side. But age has a way of inviting you to advance in maturity. So, throughout the years, we have come to realize that there are more than two sides to every story. While there is one person's side, and the other person's side, there is also a deeper side of every story—God's side. As human beings, we are limited in our ability to discern all sides to every story. We can't possibly know things such as a person's family of origin, hidden struggles, fears, weaknesses and strengths, and life experiences.

There is also a spiritual side to people's stories that is often overlooked. The Bible talks about this, saying, "For we do not wrestle against flesh and blood, but against principalities, against powers, against the rulers of the darkness of this age, against spiritual hosts of wickedness in the heavenly places."[5] The reality is we have an Enemy who is waging a battle against us. He loves to use unrighteous judgment to separate God's children. But the good news is this: We have a good Father who knows *every* side of every story. Only He can rightly discern a person's heart and motives.

Life is lived in a story

tim

I remember talking to a firefighter friend from a neighboring department about how no one can know *every* side to a story. The next time we met, he said he'd thought a lot about what we'd talked about, and he shared the following personal experience with me.

He began by saying, "Tim, you know how fire department promotion and retirement parties are a really big deal and include lots of fun and alcoholic beverages. And the unwritten rule is that if a fire officer or firefighter is off duty, they make it a top priority to attend these gatherings—right?"

"Yes," I replied, "fire department promotion/retirement parties are gatherings you are expected to be at—period!"

My friend continued, "After I got promoted a couple years ago, I was assigned to an Engine Company on a different shift. I quickly realized that everybody gossiped and slandered one firefighter who never attended promotion or retirement parties. I even jumped on the bandwagon and unrighteously judged and slandered him.

"Over time, as I worked with this firefighter, I realized he was one of the hardest working and most conscientious men on our company. In fact, we became good friends and even our families enjoyed hanging out together. Our kids invited his kids to church, and my friend ended up recommitting his life to Christ. Anyway, when the next retirement party was scheduled, I made it a point to approach my friend, in hopes that I could change his mind about not attending. I said, 'Come on; come with us. Everyone from the Engine Company is going together. We'll pick you up and all drive together.' My friend got real quiet, and said, 'Thanks, but I can't make the party.'

"This time I decided to take the conversation a little further by saying, 'Can I ask why?'

"My friend looked down at the ground and said, 'It's a long story. One that I've never talked about at work ... but I am a recovering alcoholic.' There was a long pause, and I had no idea what to say.

"My friend continued, 'The truth is that I can't go to parties where there is alcohol. I just don't trust myself. Maybe one day I will be able to do that, but not right now. So, when you guys are at the party, I'll be at an AA meeting with my sponsor.'

"He shook his head back and forth and said, 'You know, I almost lost my entire family over drinking. If it wasn't for my wife believing in me, our marriage would have been over a long time ago. She has been such an encourager. But I view this as my last chance—and I can't blow it.'

"Tim, when I heard my friend's side of the story, it was like a veil came down—I felt awful. All I thought about were the times I'd judged him and gossiped about him. I was only seeing my side of the story. I had no idea about my friend's struggles to live in freedom from an addiction that threatened to ruin him and his family."

THE HEART

Righteous judging can easily turn into unrighteous judging when a person decides to judge another person's heart or motives. The Bible says,

"God *sees* not as man sees, for man looks at the outward appearance, but the Lord looks at the heart."[6] Another passage says, "God, who knows the heart ..."[7]

We suspect some readers may be thinking, *But aren't we called to make judgments?* Our answer to that question is "yes" and "no." For example, key questions to ask when making a decision are: *Have I included God* (**I.O.T.L.**)? *Where is my heart, and what's my motive in my decision-making process?*

So, when the Scriptures warn a person to "judge not," it does not mean they can't discern and appraise whether something is right or wrong. *Judge not* means to never condemn a person or pass judgment on them. The Bible says, "He who is spiritual appraises all things."[8] That sounds good, right? But the golden question is *How does a person do that; how do they appraise all things in God-honoring ways?*

For us personally, we try to begin everything by inviting God into the conversation and into our process by inquiring of the Lord—**I.O.T.L.** Practically speaking, we try to follow the Bible verse that says, "We are taking every thought captive to the obedience of Christ."[9] We do that because we know we need God's wisdom.[10] Remember, only God knows a person's heart. He knows *every* side to a person's story; He even know the secrets in a person's heart.[11]

Unrighteous judgment also relates to the sowing-and-reaping cycle we talked about in the previous chapter. For example, let's say a person grows up unrighteously judging, dishonoring, and criticizing their parents. One day they get married and have children of their own. Imagine that they come home after a long day at work and hear their kids unrighteously judging and dishonoring them. How does the parent respond? They default to unrighteously judging their kids. And this destructive cycle continues through another generation.

A good question is *What are some practical ways to avoid unrighteous judging?* The Bible offers a solution, saying, "Finally, brethren, whatever is true, whatever is honorable, whatever is right, whatever is pure, whatever is lovely, whatever is of good repute, if there is any excellence and if anything worthy of praise, dwell on these things."[12] The wisdom and truth packed in that single verse could fill an entire book. Think about it, what if instead of unrighteously judging a person defaults to what they know rather than what they don't know—and what they may never know. Spouses who purposefully focus on, "whatever is true, whatever is honorable, whatever is right, whatever is pure, whatever is lovely, whatever is of good repute, if there is any excellence and if anything worthy of praise, dwell on these things," will advance in intimacy—and experience more regular SOUL*gasms*.

HOW ABOUT YOU?

Throughout this book, we've encouraged you to focus on what *you* can do—not on what *others* need to do. We encourage both husbands and wives to stay in their own lane by taking ownership and responsibility for the areas of their life that they alone are accountable to God for. Remember, the Bible says, "Pay close attention to yourself and to your teaching."[13]

Here is an even deeper personal challenge to consider: Do you have the *fruit* of judgment in your life? The fruit of judgment can include a long list of negative responses. For example, unrighteous judgment can harden a person's heart and leave them feeling bitter or resentful. The fruit of unrighteous judgment can leave a person feeling angry, cynical, sarcastic, and untrusting. We want to suggest that when the *fruit* of judgment is present in your life, there is often a *root* of judgment in play. Hebrews 12:15 says, "See to it that no one comes short of the grace of God; that no *root of bitterness* springing up causes trouble; and by it many be defiled."

It's been our observation that when a person tends to default to unrighteously judging others, they usually have a lot of rules for people to follow. And their rules often include a long list of *shoulds*. This becomes fertile ground for roots of bitterness to spring up in their life and relationships. And when it comes to marriage, roots of bitterness are like a nuclear explosion that negatively impacts a couple's intimacy. Bitterness can be like a cancer that *blocks* a person from enjoying *ordinary* and *extraordinary* moments—and experiencing SOUL*gasm*. Unrighteous judging can also lead to hardness of heart. Jesus warned about hardness of heart, saying Moses *permitted* divorce because the hearts of the people had hardened toward each other but he never *commanded* it.[14] Similar to unrighteous judging, hardness of heart is devastating to intimacy and limits experiencing SOUL*gasm*.

Unrighteous judgment and bitterness are based in shame, fear, control, rejection, rebellion, envy, unforgiveness, and condemnation. People who struggle with unrighteous judging often minimize this destructive cycle by saying things such as "I didn't mean anything by it; it was harmless; I was raised in a family where everyone had lots of opinions about others; this is how God wired me; I'm a leader; it's just the way I am."

JUDGING SEXUAL SIN

When it comes to sexual sin, Christians can quickly default to unrighteous judgment. Jesus addressed sexual sins, saying, "Let him who is without sin cast the first stone ... where are your accusers? ... Neither do

I condemn you ... your sins are forgiven, go and sin no more."[15] Certainly, sexual sins are *different* than other sins,[16] but they are not *worse* than other sins. However, the consequences to sexual sins can often be worse. Nonetheless, as we study the life of Jesus, He really went after what Bible interpreters call "high-handed sins." These included unrighteous judgment, pride, idolatry, arrogance, control, religiosity, and a critical spirit.

We will conclude this chapter by reminding readers that *unrighteous judging* is a serious offense that sets negative spiritual laws in motion and becomes a SOUL*gasm blocker*. Choosing not to judge sets positive spiritual laws in motion.

ARE YOU UP FOR A REAL LIFE CHALLENGE?

Take some time to study the following Bible passages: "Do not judge, or you too will be judged. For in the same way you judge others, you will be judged, and with the measure you use, it will be measured to you."[17] "Therefore you have no excuse, everyone of you who passes judgment, for in that which you judge another, you condemn yourself; for you who judge practice the same things. And we know that the judgment of God rightly falls upon those who practice such things."[18]

In closing, unlike playing the Lotto, understanding spiritual laws will bring a great return on your investment. As you advance in better understanding these laws, we pray you will make wise choices when opportunities arise. Remember, healthy people always have choices. To push back against unrighteous judging, we quote the apostle Paul who said, "Fix your thoughts on what is true and good and right. Think about things that are pure and lovely, and dwell on the fine, good things in others. Think about all you can praise God for and be glad about."[19]

CHAPTER 10

HANDLING OFFENSES POORLY

What are your favorite movies? A few of ours include *Field of Dreams* ("If you build it, they will come"); *About Time* (living every day as if it's your last); *A Few Good Men* (can you picture Jack Nicholson, the highly decorated Marine officer, in the courtroom witness chair, glaring at Tom Cruise as he barks out, "You can't handle the truth!"?); *The Mask of Zorro*, (especially when Anthony Hopkins [an old Zorro] exhorts Antonio Banderas [an emerging new Zorro], saying, "Yes, you will fight bravely—and die quickly!"); *Braveheart* ("Freedom!"); *Good Will Hunting,* (remember when Robin Williams repeats over and over to Matt Damon, "It's not your fault! It's not your fault!"?). And so many other great films, such as *Citizen Kane, Hoosiers, Lars and the Real Girl, Rocky, Raiders of the Lost Ark*, and more recently, *The Greatest Showman.*

We own most of these films, and we've watched each one a number of times. Each one averages approximately two hours in length. Therefore, if we watched a film ten times, that would involve twenty hours of movie watching. When a film impacts a person's life, he or she can recall specific scenes, certain lines, and even recognize the theme music years after watching the film. If you close your eyes, can you recall the music to *The Godfather* or *Jaws*?

Let's imagine that you were raised in a family where you (symbolically) watched the same movie play over and over. This involved 365 days a year, let's say for 20 years, which is 7,300 days. Multiply this number of days by 24 hours per day, and the result is that you watched your family movie play out for 175,200 hours! Your family-of-origin movie played nonstop, every day of your life. Perhaps you experienced, or failed to experience, healthy modeling of forgiveness and unforgiveness, pride and humility, kindness and unkindness, grace and criticalness, acceptance and rejection, fear and courage. Maybe you saw a lack of discipline or too much discipline, an attitude of superiority and comparison instead of wholeheartedly celebrating others, lack of a father figure or a hyper-controlling father figure, good or poor parenting. Families of origin issues include addictions, workaholism, alcoholism, drug problems, gambling; as well as homes that were filled with neglect, anger, resentment, rage, and abuse.

As you review your life, what was the model you had for handling offenses? The reason this topic is so important is because being able to handle offenses in a godly way positions a person to experience more peace and joy in their life. It makes room for SOUL*gasm* moments.

The truth is if you are breathing, you will be offended. Look at our culture, conservatives are offended by liberals, and vice versa. A Catholic can be offended by an Evangelical. A CRC (Christian Reformed Church) person who went to Calvin College can offend an RCA (Reformed Church of America) person who went to Hope College. A Cubs fan can offend a White Sox fan. A private-school fan can be offended by a public-school fan. An NRA member can offend a pacifist. A La Leche league member can be offended by parents who give their babies formula. A Starbucks fan can be offended by a Dunkin' Donuts fan. In all of these examples, either party can offend the other. Tragically, many people consider the card-carrying-right-wing-evangelical Christian to be one of the most offensive people in our post-Christian culture.

"WAYS"

As you observed the movie playing in your family of origin, it resulted in doing life in certain *ways*. And the truth is that eventually your *ways* will most likely offend somebody—even your spouse. The difficult part is that most people grow up believing their *way* is the right *way* and that other people who have a different way of doing life are doing it the wrong way. In marriage, couples can be offended by the way a spouse drives, parents, handles finances, makes coffee, or makes love. Even churches have their preferred ways of doing things. For example, infant baptism or baby dedication? Traditional or contemporary worship? Calvinism or Arminianism? Women elders/teachers or only men elders/teachers?

In relationships and in life, there are certain *ways* every person has—that's just the way it is! The good news is that as a person explores their ways, including how they handle offenses, it can become an invitation to live life and marriage in the Larger Story, advance in intimacy, increase in celebrating *ordinary* and *extraordinary* moments, and enjoy SOUL*gasm*.

"YOU HAVE HEARD ... BUT I TELL YOU"

In Matthew chapter 5, what is referred to as the Sermon on the Mount, Jesus gives some revolutionary teaching. He begins by saying, "You have heard," and then He tells His disciples something they've heard before. However, next Jesus uses an interesting transition; He goes from "You have heard," to "but I tell you." Jesus seemed to be saying, "You have heard"—you know the *way*; or you think you know the *way*—"But I tell you," and Jesus describes another *way*.

Jesus uses this approach a number of times, saying, "You have heard that it was said, do not commit adultery ... *but I tell you* ...

You have heard that it was said, that anyone who divorces his wife ... *but I tell you* ...

You have heard that it was said, do not break your oaths ... *but I tell you* ...

You have heard that it was said, an eye for an eye and a tooth for a tooth ... *but I tell you* ...

You have heard that it was said, love your neighbor and hate your enemy ... *but I tell you* ..."

Can we ask, *Does Jesus' style of teaching in these passages bother you?* Personally, we don't mind when people tell us things we have not heard. But when they begin by telling us things we've already heard, it makes us wonder: *Where are they going?* And when they give their perspective of things we've already heard and have our own perspectives on, it can trigger all sorts of emotions in us. All that is to say, is it possible that what the disciples *heard* wasn't what they needed to *know*? Or perhaps the *ways* we believe that we know, or the *ways* that we think we know, aren't what we need to know?

How a couple learns to handle offenses most definitely will impact the intimacy in their marriage. Our culture says when a person is offended, the way to handle it is to respond the same way. In other words—get even! An eye for an eye. If you offend me, I'll offend you. These types of responses become SOUL*gasm blockers* in marriage and in life. However, the Bible describes a revolutionary way to handle offenses. It says, "A person's wisdom yields patience; it is to one's glory to overlook an offense."[1] This way of handling offenses is so countercultural. But it is a *way* that is filled with wisdom, and leads to increased intimacy, and experiencing SOUL*gasm*.

WHAT OFFENDS THE MIND REVEALS THE HEART

Have you ever considered that *what offends the mind reveals the heart?* Our experience is that often the destiny of a person's life unfolds at the intersection of an offense. Okay, some readers may be thinking, *What's the big deal about handling offenses?* Remember, how a person responds when they are offended sets positive and negative spiritual laws in motion. The key is to not focus on the offense, but to first invite God into your process—**I.O.T.L.**—and then to follow His lead on how to respond.

Life is about story. And stories build intimacy. Everything involves story—even how you handle offenses. Remember, we said that every person's life can be lived in one of two stories, the Larger Story or the smaller story. If the main character in your story is *you*, you are living in the smaller story. And if the main character is *God*, you are living in the Larger Story. When a person is offended, if they choose to live in the smaller story, it often plays out with them responding by offending, attacking, gossiping, and slandering the person who offended them.

However, if the main character in a person's story is God, they are living in the Larger Story. When they are offended, it becomes an opportunity to **I.O.T.L.**, model reciprocal servanthood, and view others as "more important than yourself."[2] Nevertheless, we want to go on record saying that living in the Larger Story is not for the faint of heart.

Life is lived in a story

tim

I am *so* not a techy-type person. In fact, the only keys that are worn out on my keyboard are Control-Alt-Delete! A while back, I was in a jam and needed a friend to give me some important technical direction. Over the course of a few days, I called him a number of times, left several voice messages, emailed, and texted him multiple times. After not receiving any responses from my friend, let's just say my voice messages, texts, and emails got snarky and sarcastic. *Why?* Because *I was offended.*

My being offended morphed into becoming demanding and unrighteously judging my friend. I thought to myself, *I can't believe this guy is not responding to me!*

And it gets worse. When my friend continued not to respond to my emails (which turned into nasty-grams), I did what most brave-hearted American men do—I started whining to Anne. I said, "I always get back to people; I can't believe he is dismissing me like this. All I'm asking is for some technical information that he could tell me in his sleep; it might take ten minutes out of his precious schedule. If he needed something, I would drop everything and help him out. In fact, I remember when he was in a jam and I changed my plans to help him. It's not like I'm asking for his firstborn. Some friend he turned out to be." I even pontificated to my kids, saying, "I hope you don't treat your friends like this guy is treating your dear old dad!" With each day that passed without getting a response, I got more *judgy*—remember, *I was offended!* And the more I grumbled about him, the worse it got.

Then after an entire week of frustrated one-way conversations, I finally got an email from the person I now considered my ex-friend. It read, "Tim, I am so sorry I have not gotten back to you. I've been on a cruise for a week. My cell phone broke, and the ship was having problems with their internet connection so I was unable to check my emails. Sorry this took so long; attached is the information you needed. Take care, I can't wait to have lunch together, catch up, and share about this amazing trip—love ya, bud."

What offends the mind reveals the heart. I was offended and living in the smaller story where it was *all about me.* I involved my bride and kids. I gossiped and slandered. I unrighteously judged, and then my friend responds with an apology and says, *Can't wait to get together—love ya, bud.*

When I was offended, my heart was revealed. When I reviewed this situation, and processed how poorly I handled it, I thought about those seven words: *What offends the mind reveals the heart.* I remember thinking, *I need to grow in how I handle offenses. And I want to better understand how my heart has anything to do with how I handle offenses.* One Bible verse that gave me perspective says, "The mouth speaks out of that which fills the heart."[3]

Can we gently ask, *What comes out of your mouth?* If this passage is true, that *the mouth speaks out of that which fills the heart,* then if a person spews gossip, slander, anger, and contempt; then according to this passage, that person's heart is filled with gossip, slander, anger, and contempt.

How about when *you* are offended, what comes out of your mouth? Consider that what comes out of your mouth are the things that are in your heart.[4] After decades of following Jesus, frankly, we know how to play what we refer to as the "Christian game." When we are offended or triggered, most of the time we don't gossip and slander out loud, instead we go stealth. This manifests in a number of ways. For example, we can just passively ignore the person, or conveniently pass over their name on our prayer lists. We can strategically and systematically manipulate a conversation without obvious slandering. We are black-belts in *working the system* when we are offended.

But it's the sincere desire of our hearts to live in the Larger Story, with God as the main character. And while we certainly have not arrived, this continues to be a key step in our personal maturity as we make choices that require us to *grow up.*

There is tremendous power in words; they can be used to bless and to curse.[5] However, the reality is that people say mean things. And after years of counseling experiences with couples, we have observed that *wounded people wound people!*

The Bible says, "Above all else, guard your heart, for everything you do flows from it."[6] When the Bible says, *Above all else,* those three words immediately get our attention. Remember, "The mouth speaks out of that which fills the heart,"[7] and healthy people always have choices. That means we can choose to handle offenses with negativity and words that tear people down, or we can handle offenses by choosing to presuppose the best in others and use life-giving words. However, choices have consequences, and choosing words that do not presuppose the best in others can become SOUL*gasm blockers.* And choosing life-giving words can become SOUL*gasm builders.*

Sometimes handling offenses can include being sinned against. In Tim's story above, his friend never sinned against him. But when sin is in play, Matthew chapter 18 addresses specific steps for a person to take. First, you are to go to the person. Next, if they don't respond, involve one or two others and meet together with the person. If you cannot reconcile, treat the person as a tax gatherer, or in today's language, a person from the IRS. As a reminder, how did Jesus treat the tax gatherers? He loved them.

HOW ABOUT YOU?

Every person will be offended at some point, especially in marriage. The key is to first **I.O.T.L.** and bring the offense to God. Next, take ownership and responsibility for your part in the situation and relationship. If necessary, ask for forgiveness and forgive yourself. Then choose to view the offense as an *opportunity* not as an *obstacle*. And always remember that God is interested in your *heart*.[8]

$$+ + +$$

We will conclude this chapter by reminding readers that handling offenses in unkind, immoral, or dishonest ways set negative spiritual laws in motion. And handling offenses in righteous, kind, and godly ways sets positive spiritual laws in motion. And when couples handle offenses in kind and life-giving ways, it leads to increased intimacy—and experiencing SOUL*gasm*.

CHAPTER 11

FAILING TO HONOR PARENTS

As our kids were growing up, we challenged them with key Bible texts. One passage in particular involved the spiritual law surrounding honoring parents. The fifth commandment commands, "Honor your father and mother." When we talked about that passage, we reminded our children that this is the *only* one of the Ten Commandments that included a promise. As children honor parents, the Bible says, "Things will go well with you."[1] As a side note, if we overemphasized "honoring parents," one of our children would winsomely respond by saying, "Dad/Mom, doesn't the Bible also address parents—saying, *'Do not exasperate your children'?*"[2]

When it comes to marriage, couples who dishonor their parents generally come to the realization that it is a sure-fire SOUL*gasm blocker*. And couples who honor their parents recognize it as a SOUL*gasm builder*. It's been our experience that when a person honors their parents, things seem to go well with them.

Life is lived in a story

anne

Tim and I left Chicago and moved to Holland, Michigan, in July 1997. We were among the first in our large families to move out of state. Although that was more than twenty years ago, I can still vividly remember the weekend my parents came to visit us in our new home. Being together as a family is extra special when you live miles apart.

That weekend we found ways to pack plenty of living into a short amount of time. When they arrived, we walked on Lake Michigan beaches, took pictures of "Big Red" lighthouse, and enjoyed food and conversations around our table. We found time to introduce my parents to some of our new friends, and even took them downtown to shop at the quaint stores in Holland. But on Monday morning, our time had come to an end. Tim helped my dad load their car before they headed back to the Chicago suburbs.

There are many chapters in a person's life and story. Some chapters are public and enjoyed by all, others remain private. Sometimes the private chapters need time for healing and deeper understanding before a person is comfortable sharing them. For us, God used the time we'd spent living away from family to invite us to better understand the story around my family from His perspective. In order to understand the impact of this particular weekend, I will start by describing some chapters that have not been a part of our public story—until now.

Tim and I were both were raised in strong families. We grew up in the same town, a few blocks away from each other. The church we attended while growing up was the same church we got married in. For both of us, faith was a foundational part of the story God was telling through our lives and families. Looking back, after getting married at twenty-one, I would describe my early to mid-twenties as a period when I was spiritually seeking.

Growing up in a strict religious home didn't leave a lot of room to ask questions. The faith I grew up with was given to me, like an inheritance passed down from one generation to the next. But it never felt as if my faith was my own. When it came to answering deeper questions—I had few answers. At least not the kind of answers that were rooted in confidence in God. I wanted to intimately know God and understand what He expected from me. I was raised knowing how to follow the rules and color inside the lines. But it wasn't more *knowledge* about formal religion I was seeking; it was *intimacy* and *relationship* with God. Frankly, I didn't know what that looked like—or where to begin looking.

While I was unsure of many things in those early years, somewhere in my *heart*, I sensed God was big enough to handle my questions. Part of the problem was, I didn't have the same confidence in my family's ability to do the same. Which is probably a big reason why my search began later than most.

Being married provided me so much freedom to explore spiritual questions. During our early years of marriage, Tim and I were invited to attend a new church called Willow Creek that was meeting in a movie theater. Growing up Catholic, I'd never attended any other church. One day when Tim was on duty at the firehouse, I decided to accept an invitation to attend this start-up church a few miles from our home. The details that followed that Sunday are not all that important to this story, so I'll skip ahead and say that over time, that church became our community of faith for the next twenty years.

If Tim and I wrote a book about those years, it would be filled with stories about the miraculous ways God invited us to join Him. We would tell you how God revealed Himself to us in very personal ways, and how we learned the difference between *religion* and *relationship* with God. We would tell stories of how God invited us to grow up spiritually, emotionally, and relationally in more ways than we could have imagined. But what we never fully realized was the negative impact our decision to leave the Catholic Church had on my family. Leaving the church my family attended, the religion that Tim and I were raised in, is a bittersweet part of our story that resulted in years of hurt and pain.

With each passing year, our decision to go to a different church continued to be a source of strain on our relationship with my family. There was so much they didn't understand, and so much we were unable to explain. In our twenties and thirties, we lacked the maturity that I am sure would have helped make the transition smoother. For my family, our decision to leave the Catholic Church felt like a form of betrayal—as if we were turning our backs on them, and on God. From their perspectives, we were leaving behind something that was as foundational as our Irish-German-Welsh heritages. The reality is that we were all heartbroken, and no one knew how to fix it.

Any hint of conversation around spiritual things, such as church-related events or activities, became a source of pain, and was met with feelings of disapproval. Eventually, my parents requested that we not discuss those areas of our life with them. In an attempt to honor their desire, and to move forward as a family, we avoided the topics they considered off limits. While that seemed to be a temporary solution to the problem, it actually became our next problem. When we stopped discussing our spiritual lives and growing relationships with God, we felt as though we were leaving on the sidelines a huge part of who we were becoming.

Sadly, my family never attended our baptisms, or any of our children's baby dedication services. We were hardly ever asked to attend Catholic functions, such as infant baptisms, communion, or confirmation ceremonies. We were not asked to be sponsors or godparents. At family weddings and funerals, we were reminded that we should not take part in communion because we were no longer part of the Catholic Church.

For Tim and me and our families, our spiritual lives were like two ships that had left the harbor together, but then we pursued courses that were five degrees off from each other. Over time, we found ourselves miles apart. As a couple, our relationship with God was such a growing part of our lives that it was impacting who Tim and I were becoming in amazing ways. We met new friends, joined small groups, attended and led Bible studies, and spent summers serving at our church camp. We joined prayer groups, audited marriage courses at Wheaton college, joined the marriage team at Willow Creek, taught premarital seminars, and went on mission trips. But since none of these life-changing events were shared with my parents or sisters, our lives were progressively disconnecting.

But it wasn't all bad; being part of a big family meant lots of great things were also happening. Babies were born, and birthdays and holidays were celebrated. Tim was working his way up through the ranks of the fire department. By the time he was in his late thirties, he'd been promoted to Deputy Fire Chief. However, in the fast pace of that season of life, it was easy to underestimate how much damage was being done by choosing avoidance as the solution to being disconnected from my family.

In the early 1990's, a group of people from Willow Creek moved to Holland, Michigan, to plant a church. A few years later, they called Tim and offered him a full-time, paid staff position. Tim accepted a position that the world would consider a demotion. We referred to it as *downward mobility* as we took a substantial pay cut and forfeited benefits that accompanied a twenty-plus-year, fire department career. But from our perspective, we sensed God was inviting us to *trust* and *risk*—and take this leap of faith.

So, as I fast-forward to our move to Holland, perhaps, you can better understand why having my parents stay at our house that weekend created a dynamic that we'd learned how to avoid when we lived in the Chicago suburbs. Since my mom and dad never attended church with us or participated in any faith-based events outside the Catholic Church, Tim and I anticipated some awkward moments during their visit. When Sunday arrived, we asked them if they would like to go to our church or attend the nearby Catholic Church—they chose the latter.

At the time, two of our four children were attending Hope College. While my parents were visiting that weekend, one of our daughters innocently invited them to attend the college chapel service on Monday morning. The invitation was followed by an awkward silence. But, like so many awkward silences in the past, we learned how to move past it and redirect the conversation toward a different topic.

On Monday morning, we were walking my parents to the car to say goodbye, when my dad suddenly announced, "Mom and I would like to stop by Hope College's chapel service and say goodbye to the girls before we head home." My jaw almost dropped to the ground. *Did my dad just say they were going to drop by Hope chapel?* Without skipping a beat, we acted like that was *completely normal*. We jumped into our car and told them to follow us to the college. Tim and I didn't say very much to each other in the car. Instead, we prayed the entire way. Pulling into the parking lot, the four of us headed toward Dimnent Chapel, which is in the heart of the campus.

My heart was beating out of my chest. We arrived a few minutes late, and the chapel was filled beyond capacity. Students were seated on the floor in the main aisle. The balcony and side aisles were standing-room only. The worship was winding down, and a few students were kind enough to give us their seats. Tim and I squeezed into the pew and sat directly behind my mom and dad. The chaplain moved to the center of the stage and began speaking. "Today's reading will be out of the book of Deuteronomy, chapter five, verse sixteen. 'Honor your father and mother.'" He went on to say, "Did you know that the fifth commandment is the only commandment of the Ten Commandments with a promise? The Bible challenges us to 'Honor your father and mother,' and the text concludes, saying, 'so it will go well with you.'" I squeezed Tim's hand, knowing God had something planned for that morning, but I had absolutely no idea what it was.

Chapel services are always short. Within twenty minutes, students were filing out of the packed church. We congregated in the vestibule and waited for the kids to join us. The girls ran up to my parents, thanked them for coming to chapel, and gave them one more hug before heading off to class. The next thing I remember was how odd it felt for the four of us to be standing together in the back of a non-Catholic church.

Just as my parents were moving toward the exit, Tim spoke in a serious tone, "Gram, Papa, could I talk to you for a moment before you head out?" Tim is known for his lighthearted personality, so when he uses his serious voice, people lean in to listen. I had no idea what he wanted to talk to my parents about, but I had a sense it was important.

Tim paused and took a deep breath before he began. I remember glancing over at him, because I sensed that he was about to get emotional. This is what I remember next: Tim began by saying, "This morning's message about honoring your parents reminded me of my mom and dad. You know, they've been gone almost five years now. It's still hard for me to believe how much life has happened in those years. I left the fire department, and we moved to Holland—a town they will never see." His eyes began to well with tears. "It's hard to think about our kids attending college and knowing my parents will not share this part of their lives." Pausing to compose himself, he said, "I really miss them. Which is just one reason you attending chapel service with us today means the world to Anne and me."

My parents smiled. But they appeared uncomfortable about what may be coming next. Tim continued, "You know, when Anne and I got married, we never planned on leaving the Catholic Church. And we weren't looking for another church or denomination. We never imagined how painful our decision would be for you both."

[Sidebar: I come from a long line of "conflict-avoiders." So, as Tim was speaking, I could see my mom's conflict-avoiding detectors being activated.] My mom tried several times to interrupt in order to move the conversation in another direction. At one point she said, "Now, Tim, it's been a lovely weekend, Dad and I enjoyed seeing the kids and your new home, and you know we love you and Annmarie. Now don't get yourself upset; we're all fine now. Jack, we better get going if we are going to beat the traffic."

Tim was determined to finish. He looked directly into my mom's eyes and said, "Gram—please, let me finish." My dad nodded his head for Tim to continue. Tim took a deep breath and said, "I guess, no matter how much time has passed, or how *fine* we are now, I want you to know that our decision to attend a different church was never meant to hurt you. It was never meant to be a sign of disrespect, or a judgment about you as parents. When you asked us to avoid talking about church or spiritual things, it felt like everything started to deteriorate from there. Before you head back home, I want to say that I wish I'd found a way to push through and communicate what was happening spiritually to Anne and me. As I look back, I think we could have done a better job of walking that out with you. I think, over time, as our relationship went south, I just pulled back. I want to say I am sorry, I was wrong—will you forgive me?"

Without a word spoken, my mom and dad both nodded slowly.

"Second," Tim continued, "as I think about our relationship, I've always enjoyed doing things for you. I could take your car to the firehouse to wash and wax it, shovel your driveway, or mow your lawn. But looking back, all of that was pretty easy for me. But what I didn't do with you, and what I needed to do, was to engage with you emotionally. I think I was just trying to protect myself. And I chose not to give you my heart. I just want to say I am sorry. I was wrong to do that. Will you forgive me?"

Again, they both nodded, but didn't say a word.

Tears began to roll down Tim's cheeks. He took another deep breath and pushed through his emotion. "I want to apologize for one more thing. You both knew my dad and mom, you know how much I loved them, and how much I miss them."

My parents nodded somberly.

"As the relationship between the four of us got more complicated, I never felt comfortable referring to you as *Mom* or *Dad*. I guess those titles meant so much to me, and not using them was my way of withholding my heart from you. When the kids came along, we all focused our attention on them. So, it was easy to call you 'Gram' and 'Papa.' I am really sorry that I didn't love you in the ways I know I could have. Will you forgive me for that?"

"Of course, we forgive you, Tim," my mom replied.

Tim looked them both directly in their eyes, and said, "One last thing, before you get in the car and head home, if it's not too late, can I start calling you 'Mom' and 'Dad'?"

Tears were flowing down my cheeks. I looked at my dad, and his lips were quivering. My mom was trying to hold back emotion. My mom spoke for both of them, and she said, "Tim, that would be wonderful—Dad and I would love that—wouldn't we, Dad?" My father nodded.

We all hugged each other, walked to the car, and waved goodbye. Tim and I stood in the parking lot for what seemed to be a very long time after their car pulled away. Tears ran down our cheeks as we held each other. There were no words exchanged between us as we experienced such an extraordinary SOUL*gasm* moment.

God completely surprised Tim and me that weekend with a miracle that I had prayed for since the day we told my parents we were leaving the Catholic Church. And then, in an instant, as we sat in a college chapel service, God invited us to join Him. He invited Tim to trust Him and take a risk—and Tim said *yes*.

My dad died a few years later. My mom lived another thirteen years after his passing. As I write this story, the memories of my parents that I hold closest to my heart are the years that followed that Monday morning at Hope College in Dimnent Chapel. In response to a twenty-minute service, everything changed between us. Years of distance and misunderstanding started to melt away. God began to *build* a bridge between us that grew stronger in the years that followed.

After that encounter, we connected with my parents in ways we never imagined were possible. And every time I heard Tim call them "Mom" and "Dad," I could sense the joy in their hearts—and in ours. A few years later, my dad was admitted to hospice, and Tim and I were sitting at his bedside. There was something on my heart that I wanted to ask my dad, but I was afraid, because in the past, spiritual issues were such a source of pain. But it was time, and since we were now free to talk about God, I trusted God, and risked asking my dad if he would give Tim and me a father's blessing. My dad was never all that comfortable with conversations like that, nor was he generous with encouragement. But to his credit, he agreed and prayed a simple prayer over us.

What happened at Dimnent Chapel that morning was the beginning of an important chapter of truly honoring my parents. Before that day, we had all made choices that had consequences. And those consequences cost us something—years of celebrating life together that we were never able to get back.

I tell you this story to encourage you, it's never too late to do the right thing. The fifth commandment challenges people to honor parents. Trust us, dishonoring parents is a SOUL*gasm blocker*. For sons and daughters who honor parents, the Bible promises, "Things will go well with you."[3] As we honored my mom and dad, things did go well for us.

The Dimnent Chapel story is one we do not share very often. On occasions when we have, inevitably people approach us and say things such as "Are you saying I have to apologize and make amends with my parents, or call them 'Mom' or 'Dad'? Because you have absolutely *NO* idea the hurt and pain they have caused me!"

We are *not* telling anyone to do anything. We are simply sharing a story about our personal experience. We understand the importance of healthy boundaries in every relationship—even with a spouse, parents, and children. We've worked with people who have endured both active and passive negative behaviors. And we've worked with people who have been discounted, discouraged, disrespected, manipulated, abused, and denied love by their parents.

What we *are* suggesting is that you include God—**I.O.T.L.** Revisit the fifth commandment, "Honor your father and mother." As you do, the Bible says, "Things will go well with you."[4] And as you invite God into your process, if something comes to your heart or mind, to use one of our core Evans' family goals, we challenge you to "trust and risk"—trust God and take a risk.

We encourage you to invite God to show you specific ways you can honor your parents. For readers who have difficult relationships with parents, we understand parent/children relationships can be complicated. Part of growing up includes taking ownership and responsibility. Sometimes that means apologizing for ways you dishonored your parents. Saying you are sorry for things you did knowingly (sins of commission). A deeper step in honoring parents includes taking ownership and responsibility and apologizing for ways you failed to honor your parents (sins of omission).

That said, if the situation includes toxic or abusive parents, our encouragement is to prayerfully take potential next steps on a case-by-case basis. There are many ways to describe abuse, including verbal, psychological, emotional, physical, sexual, and spiritual abuse. Whether it threatens to harm a person's physical body, or causes mental anguish, or results in passive neglect—it is an issue of control. Bottom line, abuse is a violation against the human soul.

In an abusive parent situation, we encourage the son/daughter to include wise counsel, go slow, and remember that their safety is always the top priority. If the relationship continually defaults to being toxic, establish and maintain healthy boundaries. One way to honor parents from a distance is to faithfully pray for them. If a person continues to be exposed to abuse, it opens up the possibility of being re-victimized. In addition, abusive treatment can be accompanied by signs of post-traumatic stress syndrome (PTSD). Remember, forgiveness may begin with a *decision*— but healing is a *journey*.

And likewise, if you are a parent, **I.O.T.L.** and invite God to show you any next steps to take in moving toward your children in kind and life-giving ways. Is there anything the Lord may be bringing to your heart—words or actions or a specific situation—that indicates you may need to seek forgiveness from your children? Remember, our forgiveness model includes three simple steps: Step 1. *I am sorry for* [name the offense]. Step 2. *I was wrong.* Step 3. *Will you forgive me?*

If you are a person who has been blessed with great parents, ask God to show you one specific way you can honor them this week. Then trust God—and take a risk. And if your parents have died, or if honoring your parents triggers you with inordinate feelings of grief, sadness, or anger, we encourage you to talk to someone about your emotions.

The title of this book is SOUL*gasm*. As we were working on the Dimnent Chapel story, we recalled a number of intense emotions we experienced that morning. Back then, we did not refer to these feelings as SOUL*gasm*, but we remember experiencing feelings of joy, hope, gratitude, happiness, pleasure, tenderness, and excitement—emotions we currently use to describe SOUL*gasm*, and what we hope you will experience in your life and marriage.

CHAPTER 12

CHOOSING PRIDE OVER HUMILITY

In this chapter, we will explore the spiritual law related to pride and humility. These are things every person struggles with. Pride is a root issue that can seriously *block* a couple from advancing in intimacy, oneness, and experiencing SOUL*gasm*. It's such an important topic that pride has been referred to as one of the seven deadly sins. Understanding its impact and choosing humility will positively impact the intimacy between a husband and wife.

There was a hit TV show in the sixties called, "I Dream of Jeannie." It was a fantasy sitcom starring Barbara Eden, who played a genie who lived in a bottle. Larry Hagman played the role of astronaut Major Anthony Nelson. When he released the genie from the bottle, she referred to him as "master." One of the best moments of this sitcom was whenever Major Nelson asked Jeannie for anything, she would fold her arms across her chest, blink both eyes, and *voila*—he would receive whatever he asked for.

The Old Testament chronicles a somewhat similar story, saying,

> That night God appeared to Solomon and said to him, "Ask for whatever you want me to give you." Solomon

answered God, "You have shown great kindness to David my father and have made me king in his place. Now, Lord God, let your promise to my father David be confirmed, for you have made me king over a people who are as numerous as the dust of the earth. Give me *wisdom* and *knowledge*, that I may lead this people, for who is able to govern this great people of yours?"

God said to Solomon, "Since this is your heart's desire and you have not asked for wealth, possessions or honor, nor for the death of your enemies, and since you have not asked for a long life but for wisdom and knowledge to govern my people over whom I have made you king, therefore wisdom and knowledge will be given you. And I will also give you wealth, possessions and honor, such as no king who was before you ever had and none after you will have."[1]

CHOOSING PRIDE OR HUMILITY

The Bible talks a lot about pride and humility. Interestingly, not one time does the Bible frame pride in a positive light. Following are a few passages about pride and humility: "Whoever exalts himself shall be humbled; and whoever humbles himself shall be exalted."[2] "All of you, clothe yourselves with humility toward one another, for God is opposed to the proud, but gives grace to the humble. Therefore humble yourselves under the mighty hand of God, that He may exalt you at the proper time."[3]

If you research nonfiction books written about humility, you will not find all that many. One classic is *Humility* by Andrew Murray.[4] Another is written by one of our spiritual fathers, Dr. C. Peter Wagner. His book is also titled *Humility*. Following are a number of highlights from Peter Wagner's *Humility* book.[5]

Five Signposts Along the Road to Pride:

1-Yearning for human praise and accolades.

2-Keeping score.

3-Cultivating a creator complex.

4-Rejoicing in others' failures and resenting others' successes.

5-Compulsively defending yourself against criticism.

Ten Signposts Along the Road to Humility:

1-Carefully adhering to the Biblical rules for submission.

2-Understanding the role of the Holy Spirit in your daily life.

3-Discovering your spiritual gifts.

4-Knowing your place in the Body.

5-Knowing the difference between your strengths and weaknesses.

6-Daring to be realistic about your successes and failures.

7-Taking risks.

8-Accepting praise but rejecting flattery.

9-Avoiding living in the achievements of the past.

10-Having the ability to pass on your glory to others.

And Dr. Wagner lists nine ways to turn adversity into advantage:

1-Keep the long-range view.

2-Admit that your critics may be right.

3-Love the Bride.

4-Carefully choose your battles.

5-Always think the best of others.

6-Pick winners and ride out the rough spots.

7-Plan on winning some and losing some.

8-Obey the Lord.

9-Activate your *Prayer Shield*.

There are certain books in our library that have impacted us so deeply and were such an important part of our mentoring that we read them often. Dr. C. Peter Wagner's *Humility* book is one of them.

Life is lived in a story

tim

About five years into our marriage, we signed up for an intimacy-*building* course led by a Christian counselor and his wife. At our first meeting, a group of single and married adults gathered together in an office. Part of the introduction included reviewing the importance of maintaining confidentiality, going over meeting dates and times, and laying a few ground rules. Each person agreed to: (1) complete the required weekly reading assignment; and (2) answer the questions at the end of each lesson. The leaders explained the importance of every person taking ownership and responsibility to complete their work. They finished by saying if a person chose not to complete the work, they were welcome to be part of the group, but they would be restricted from participating in the group discussion. Everyone agreed to the ground rules.

That season of my life was really full; we had a four-year-old, a two-year-old, and a new baby. Between the firehouse and my side job, I was working more than seventy hours a week. Plus, I served at church and participated on two softball teams. As far as our group, it took a lot of energy for me to do the assigned reading and answer the questions.

Despite my hectic schedule, I really enjoyed the course, and Anne and I were able to connect with most of the people. However, do you ever have an *irregular person* in a group that seems to trigger you? In this group there was a woman I will refer to as "Brandie" who did that to me. At the time, I described to Anne that I felt like Brandie was not fully invested in the group. She was about five years older than us, and to me, she had an extremely laid back, laissez-faire demeanor. As I unrighteously judged her, I jokingly referred to her as "Brandie-the-hippie."

Often when our meetings began, Brandie would casually mention to the group that she did not have time to read the assignment or answer the questions. That was okay, but what bugged me was, she would verbally participate in the question-and-answer time, a clear violation of our agreed upon rule that if a person did not do the homework, they were to remain quiet.

After a few weeks of Brandie stating that she did not complete her assignment and then participating in the discussion, I became frustrated. Frankly, I was triggered by Brandie, and disappointed that our leaders did not remind her about the clear ground rules. Looking back, one week was particularly stressful for me. I'd had three busy twenty-four-hour shifts at the firehouse, the kids were sick, my side job was stressful, and Anne and I were not tracking well. But even with the crazy week, I pulled up my boots, took ownership and responsibility, and invested the time and energy to finish my reading assignment and answer the questions, which would enable me to participate in our group discussion time.

Sunday evening rolled around and as our group began, once again Brandie began by casually mentioning that she did not have time to finish the lesson. I looked to our leaders to say something and review the rules. Since they remained quiet, I said, "Before we continue, can I say something?"

"Sure, Tim," our leaders replied.

I continued, "If I recall correctly, when our group began we all agreed to do the assigned homework. And we all agreed that if a group member did *not* do the assignments, they were to remain quiet during the discussion time—is that correct?"

"Yes, that's correct," our leaders replied.

I looked at Brandie and said, "As I review three of the past four weeks, at the beginning of our meetings you have shared that you did *not* finish the assignment, and yet you participated in every week's discussion. Personally, this week has been extremely stressful for me, and it took a lot of effort for me to complete our assignment so I could participate in the discussion. And as the meeting began tonight, once again you say that you did not finish the assignment. And I suspect you plan to fully participate in our discussion time. Can you help me understand why everyone else in the group follows the agreed upon rules for participation, and you make yourself an exception to the rules?" Then I looked at our group leaders and said, "Frankly, I'm a little ticked off that you don't enforce the rules *you* established—and *everyone* agreed to follow!"

The room got extremely quiet, I saw our leaders looking at each other as if to say, *Do you want to respond or should I?* However, before either of the leaders said a word, Brandie interjected and said, "I'd like to respond to Tim—if that's okay?"

"Sure," the leaders replied.

Brandie began with a long, pregnant pause. She took a couple deep breaths and cocked her head to one side. She looked me directly in the eyes and firmly said, "You know what, Tim, as long as you are sharing what *you* think, let me share with you what *I* think. I think it would be a good idea if one week you did *not* do your homework!"

I was so stunned at Brandie's response that my mind went totally blank. The group awkwardly continued, and I felt myself completely shut down. Every time I thought about letting Brandie have it, something in my gut told me to remain silent. As the meeting concluded, I was the first to leave. Anne and I drove home, barely saying a word to each other.

Looking back, at the time I wholeheartedly believed what I was saying to Brandie was something she needed to hear. And if I took my case to a court of law, I am confident the judge would have ruled in my favor. But as time went on, the Lord brought that example back to my mind at different times until I began to see it through His eyes. I came to the realization that what I was saying came from a prideful, wounded, performance-based place in my heart. I was not confronting Brandie from a place of humility and unconditional love. I didn't know Brandie—or her story. And I certainly was not presupposing the best in her; even though I pridefully expected others to presuppose the best in me.

I believe that following rules and working hard are not bad things. But for me, I can default to being prideful, hyper-disciplined, and inordinately focus on my to-do lists. Granted, I may be able to accomplish more than many people. But the downside for me is this style of relating can result in pride, unrighteous judgment, failing to presuppose the best in others, and not living humbly or loving people well.

Another lesson I continue to learn is that my pride and performance-driven lifestyle can be rooted in an orphan-like place, rather than in a place of sonship. An orphan lifestyle is one that is defined by independence and mistrust. Orphans are on their own, they figure out life without the support of a family. On the other hand, living life as a *beloved* son includes seeing myself (and others) as God does. And rather than concentrating on what I am "doing," I remind myself who God says I am, and who He is inviting and empowering me to become. This involves stepping into my true identity—as God's *beloved* son—and regularly reminding myself that I do not have to "do" anything to make God love me more. Truth be told, there is nothing any of us can *do* to make God love us more.

That incident occurred more than thirty-five years ago, and I cannot tell you how many times the Holy Spirit has gently said to me, *Tim, maybe it would be a good idea if you didn't pridefully follow every rule to the letter of the law, worry so much about other people's behaviors, and default to unrighteously judging people.*

Looking back, I smile when I think about how God used a woman I referred to as "Brandie-the hippie" to help me see a prideful part of myself that needed to be worked on. The reality is that I continue to "do" things. But thankfully, I am also growing in putting on God's mantle of humility, and just "being" with God, Anne, and others. And sometimes, when I get triggered by someone or something, Anne smiles and gently whispers, "Tim, I'm wondering what Brandie might say about working so hard?"

+ + +

Let's revisit the story about God saying to Solomon, "Ask for whatever you want me to give you." Solomon asked for wisdom and knowledge, and God gave Solomon what he asked for. In addition, God said:

> Since this is your heart's desire and you have not asked
> for wealth, possessions or honor, nor for the death of
> your enemies, and since you have not asked for a long
> life but for wisdom and knowledge to govern my people
> over whom I have made you king, therefore wisdom and
> knowledge will be given you. And I will also give you
> wealth, possessions and honor, such as no king who was
> before you ever had and none after you will have.[6]

Solomon was the wisest person who ever lived. People still say, "She/he has the wisdom of Solomon." Solomon accumulated untold amounts of wealth and possessions. He also acquired thousands of concubines and entered into mixed marriages, which were forbidden. After being given wisdom and knowledge, and having a lifetime of successes, Solomon became filled with pride. Tragically, he did not finish his life well, in fact, many Bible interpreters believe he killed himself.

After accumulating enormous wealth and experiencing countless victories, Solomon took the bait of Satan, which is pride. And the results were catastrophic. We have tried to learn lessons from the life of Solomon. To be honest, nearly every day of our lives, we ask God for humility. Whenever we ask for God's blessings and favor, when we ask for *what God wants for us*, we regularly attach to our prayer something like, "Lord, if You give us things we ask for, as well as things You want for us—only give them to us if You give us Your mantle of humility for us to walk them out." Regarding marriage, as we **I.O.T.L.** and focus on choosing humility, both lead to increased intimacy and experiencing SOUL*gasm*.

HOW ABOUT YOU?

Every person will be tempted by pride; a key to resisting pride is to focus on humility. The Bible says, "Whoever exalts himself shall be humbled, and whoever humbles himself shall be exalted."[7] It also says, "Clothe yourselves with humility ..."[8] Can we ask, *Who dressed you today?* We are confident that you put your own clothes on. Therefore, we challenge you, every day as you put on your clothes, ask God to clothe you with His mantle of humility.

The Bible says, "The fear of the LORD is the beginning of wisdom."[9] When we read that God is "opposed to the proud,"[10] it brings a measure of fear of God into our souls. *Why?* Because we all struggle with pride. And we do not want God to "oppose us"—*yikes!* Thankfully, the remedy to pride is humility. We will conclude this chapter by reminding readers that the spiritual law surrounding pride and humility sets positive and negative things in motion.

CHAPTER 13

STUCK IN OVERDRIVE—THE FAST PACE OF LIFE

A chapter titled *Stuck in Overdrive—the Fast Pace of Life* would not have been part of marriage books published a few decades ago. Nevertheless, throughout our counseling experiences, we have seen how the pace of people's lives, schedules, increasing amounts of stress, and perfectionist tendencies can become SOUL*gasm blockers*.

The reality is we live in a season of history where there are unlimited ways to connect with people 24 hours a day, 7 days a week. These ways include cell phones, texting, Twitter, Instagram, emails, Facebook, Snapchat, and the latest social media craze. While there are many benefits that accompany social media, there is also a downside that results in people having significantly less face-to-face time with a spouse or others.

Life is lived in a story

anne

Tim and I were recently in a restaurant, and a family walked in and took the table across from where we were sitting. It looked like a mom, dad, and three pre-teen to mid-teen children. As we were enjoying our conversation, we noticed how quiet their table was. When I glanced their way, I noticed that every member in the family was on their cell phones, texting or scrolling through their screen devices. It was so interesting to us that Tim and I switched our conversation and started to guess who would talk first.

The waitress approached their table, and each person placed their order without ever actually looking at her. After placing their orders, no one uttered a word to each other. Approximately ten minutes went by, and their food arrived. The kids looked up, grabbed their plates, and starting eating. The parents likewise began to eat, again without a word—it was incredible! Finally, the daughter spoke and said, "Dad, pass me the catsup." The dad handed her the ketchup without saying a word. Each family member finished eating; there was some small talk about stopping to pick something up on the way home. As they all stood up and were getting ready to leave, the dad smiled and announced to the kids, "Okay, whose turn is it to pick the restaurant for next week's *family night*?"

Thankfully, we know others who make meal time a priority. One family we know instituted "Taco Tuesday" family nights. Another family has "Friday Meal and Movie" nights. Both families enforce one important rule: NO phones, tablets, computers, or screen devices can be used during their scheduled time together. The feedback Tim and I get from parents—and children—regarding screen-free family time is extremely positive. Makes me wonder: *Is it possible that contrary to many young adults' demands and claims, maybe they long for boundaries related to their communication devices and technological freedom?*

Okay, this might be a long shot, but could there be wisdom in the old adage that *less can be more*? Is it possible that *working smarter can trump working harder*? Is it a worthwhile investment to strategically schedule time for rest, recreation, romance, sports, hobbies—and even *play*? We have a friend who defines play as, "Rest without guilt or excuse."[1]

ARE YOU UP FOR A REAL LIFE CHALLENGE?

For three months, commit to a date night with your spouse at least every two weeks and a weekly family meal time with NO phones or electronic devices. Make these dates and gatherings a top priority for your life, family, and schedule. Then review how you advanced in intimacy—and in experiencing SOUL*gasm*—as a couple and as a family. And if you experience positive benefits, commit to another three months. Or how about scheduling regular dates with your spouse and weekly family meal times for the rest of your lives?

Okay, we suspect some readers may be thinking to themselves, *You have absolutely NO idea how busy our lives are! Our kids are involved in school, sports, music lessons, dance, church, and other extra-curricular activities. At different ages, they have different places they need to be—and guess who has to drive them—me and my spouse! Plus, we're supposed to schedule regular "date nights"—are you serious? There are just not enough hours in a day!*

Yes, we are serious. Throughout our marriage we've come to realize that a balanced life that includes rest, recreation, romance, and play can result in accomplishing more in in less time in more joyful ways. We purposefully try to avoid attempting to grind our way through life's schedules and demands. Remember, every person has the same twenty-four hours each day. How you spend yours is a choice.

When we talk about priorities and boundaries with clients, we remind them that, "Healthy people can make healthy choices, and no one is a victim to their schedules." We encourage people to take ownership and responsibility to create healthy boundaries. And we give them permission to say *no* to opportunities and demands. We challenge you to say *no* to even *good* things, and focus on saying *yes* to *God* things. Our experience has shown us that keeping priorities straight, living life with healthy boundaries, and navigating in healthy ways the enormous amount of changes in our culture will result in countless blessings and benefits.[2]

Life is lived in a story

anne

As Tim and I choose to reset the pace of our life by purposefully scheduling times for rest, recreation, romance, and play, we are often surprised at how God meets us where we are. A while back, we had a really important decision to make relating to REAL LIFE Ministries. We prayed, fasted, and felt an inordinate amount of pressure about which way we should go. After a number of days feeling stressed out about this decision, Tim suggested we take a break and go for a hike in the mountains. I initially pushed back and said we needed to make this important decision *before* we went on a hike!

Fortunately, I married someone who knows how to work hard *and* play hard. So Tim insisted we take a break and head out to our favorite Red Rock trail. I reluctantly agreed. We put on our hiking boots and headed to the mountains. Whenever we hike, we love to pray. On that particular day, we **I.O.T.L.** and asked for wisdom relating to the decision we needed to make. Halfway into our hike, we paused to take a break and enjoy the scenery. Looking at each other to share a thought, we both said we sensed God saying the exact same thing to each of us regarding the decision we were so stressed out about making.

We returned to our office and I commented to Tim, "Isn't it amazing how we've been working so hard trying to make this important decision, but it was when we took a break, put a pause on work, and hiked together that God spoke to us and we enjoyed a SOUL*gasm* moment?"

We can both run at fairly high RPMs. We have a history of pulling up our boots, pushing through, and getting the job done. But as we've entered our sixties, we are realizing more and more that when we cease striving and try to work smarter not harder, when we focus on living out our *true identities* as God's *beloved* daughter and son, and when we strategically invest in rest, recreation, romance, refreshment and play, God meets us and provides what we have always worked so hard to obtain on our own.

For us, living a balanced life includes having healthy boundaries. But maintaining boundaries requires God's help. It means we have to grow up and act like adults. This looks like learning to say *no* to people when *no* isn't what they want to hear. Learning to be okay being misunderstood. Learning to trust God for direction when common sense may indicate something else. Maintaining healthy boundaries means we have to take responsibility for our priorities, schedules, decisions, and choices.

Regarding boundaries, throughout the year Anne leads a five-week co-dependency course for women. Some of the topics they discuss include identifying how you function in your family, finding your voice, and maintaining healthy boundaries. At the conclusion of the course, she hands out five-by-five wooden plaques that have the word "NO" carved on them. She reminds the women that "NO can be a complete sentence." God has used her co-dependency course to reinforce healthy behaviors in our own marriage and life, such as learning how to say NO and maintain boundaries. Again, *inquiring of the Lord* (**I.O.T.L.**) is where we begin our decision-making process as we implement the **Traffic Light Principle**.

And if we *both* do not have a "green light" from the Lord, we are getting more confident in saying *no* without feeling that we have to provide an explanation as to why. For couples who are looking for ways to remove the SOUL*gasm blockers* that threaten their intimacy, John Eldredge says it well:

> If you want to make room in your soul for God, you have to let go of all the things that are currently filling your soul. You might be surprised by how much is filling your soul. So, we give it all back to Him—we give everyone, and everything back to Jesus. The fruit of this practice has become so life giving, I do it now several times a day.[3]

Growing up means taking ownership and responsibility for yourself, your life, and your marriage by investing in healthy rest, recreation, romance, refreshment, and play—without any shame, guilt, or excuses. Scheduling these practices are some of the most important appointments on our calendars. In fact, to help us practically walk out a balanced life, every month we schedule a "D.O.F." (Day-of-Fun). Tim typically runs point on these. They can include sleeping in, hiking or a drive in the mountains, going to see a film, a short motorcycle ride, enjoying a good meal, or having great sex. The options are limitless when it comes to finding ways to *build* SOUL*gasm* moments.

ARE YOU UP FOR A REAL LIFE CHALLENGE?

We challenge every husband and wife for three months to commit to monthly Days-of-Fun. Each of you make a list of three possible days-of-fun activities you would enjoy. Together, review the six you came up with, agree on three, and view these as top life-marriage-schedule priorities. After three months, review how you advanced in spirit + soul + body oneness, celebrated *ordinary* and *extraordinary* moments, and experienced SOUL*gasm*. If you enjoyed positive benefits, commit to another three months, or how about including a monthly D.O.F. for the rest of your lives? As a side note, these are the types of questions found in our SOUL*gasm Companion Journal* (available on Amazon).

GETTING IT RIGHT

One predictable strategy the Enemy uses to *block* people from living with greater joy is increasing their stress. Often what drives their stress is rooted in a desire for perfection. When a person identifies perfectionism in their life, they often discover the roots are related to shame, fear, control, rebellion, and rejection. Perfectionistic tendencies can often be traced in a person's family line.[4]

Our culture reinforces the wrong belief that a person's security and significance comes from *doing* things and acquiring more *stuff*. This can include the size of a person's paycheck, their position, or title. The endless list includes home, cars, education, vacations, toys, the perfect body, or the latest and greatest *thing* that our culture deems valuable.

Not only are we encouraged to do more and have more, but there is an expectation that it must be done *perfectly*. Chasing this goal often gives a person a false sense of control. Perfectionism is a distraction from living the way God intends. It *blocks* joy and inhibits a couple from celebrating the deep soul connection God intended. We have allowed our culture to determine what success looks like. And we see marriages suffering because of it.

We are reminded of the story of the wise Zen Master who was beginning a new class to help students reach enlightenment. One student in particular was extremely zealous and hyper-disciplined. After a week or so, he approached the master after class and said, "How long will it take me to reach enlightenment?"

"Five years," the master replied.

"But, Master, if I am the first student to class and the last one to leave; if I do all my studies and turn in all my assignments early ... Master, if I do everything that you ask, how long will it take me to reach enlightenment?"

"Ten years."

God designed a person to get their security and significance met in Him. In other words, there is nothing you can do or achieve to make God love you more. That simple yet profound truth can positively impact a person's marriage by increasing a couple's joy and positioning them for deeper intimacy.

PART THREE

SOUL*gasm* NEXT STEPS

"One can choose to go back toward safety or forward toward growth.

Growth must be chosen again and again; fear must be overcome again and again."

Abraham H. Maslow

CHAPTER 14

LEAVING A LEGACY

In our Introduction, we gave you a little background on the word SOUL*gasm*. And while we admitted it couldn't be found in *Webster's* dictionary, we explained that it was a shared human experience. We said that SOUL*gasm* was a *response* to a person, place, or thing that can be described in a variety of ways. But at the same time, it's unique to each person. We said that some people describe it as a physical response, like an intense surge of joy that pulses through a person's entire body. Others describe it as an emotional response, much like a gentle wash of tenderness. And while God designed these to be experienced by every human being, we explained to readers that the focus of our book was on SOUL*gasm* in marriage. And we suggested that a key to enjoying SOUL*gasm* moments is to live in the present—the *now*.

In Part One, we focused on **SOUL*gasm* BUILDERS**. We encouraged husbands and wives to review steps of intimacy, recognize the influence of your family of origin, celebrate your spouse's uniqueness, consider the difference between roles and functions, and practice love and respect. We concluded Part One sharing about SOUL*gasm* sex.

In Part Two, we focused on **SOULgasm BLOCKERS**. This section included topics that often prevent couples from enjoying deeper intimacy. We encouraged husbands and wives to consider the impact of sowing and reaping, unrighteous judging, handling offenses poorly, failing to honor parents, choosing pride over humility, and being stuck in overdrive–the fast pace of life.

In Part Three, we will introduce a number of **NEXT STEPS**. This section will encourage husbands and wives to be intentional about leaving a legacy. And we will describe what we believe is the secret ingredient in marriage.

We are both in our early sixties and are at a place in life where we talk about the legacy we want to leave to our children, grandchildren, family, and friends. As much as we fully enjoy life and love being married, we know there will come a time when this earthly relationship will end, and we will say goodbye to each other and to loved ones. When that day comes, we not only want to leave individual legacies, but a life-giving marriage legacy as well. Doesn't everyone want their life to matter and make a positive impact on the world? That desire is admirable, but the truth is it's easy to lose sight of that goal in ordinary, day-to-day living.

As we saw in our last chapter, we live in a fast-paced world. Most people hit the ground running every morning and fall into bed exhausted at the end of their day. People have become so accustomed to the accelerated pace of life that they begin to actually believe they have plenty of time to relax and breathe, smell the roses, right any wrongs, say *I'm sorry* to others, love others more deeply, and leave a life-giving legacy.

This chapter is both an invitation and a challenge for every reader. An invitation to soberly evaluate your life and a challenge to seriously consider this question: *What kind of legacy do I want to leave when my life is over?* Throughout the book we've said, *Life is lived in a story and stories build intimacy.* God is telling a story through your life. Every person's life story includes a legacy that extends to children, grandchildren, and future generations.

Legacies have a number of components. One tells a story about a person's spiritual life. Another tells a story about relational, emotional, and financial decisions and behaviors. Legacies also tell stories about the choices a person made as a parent, grandparent, and friend. And when a person chooses to marry, they will one day leave behind a marital legacy.

GENERATIONAL LEGACY

When couples invest in a marriage intensive, we take an overview of their lives and marriage. We begin by exploring a person's family line going back three to four generations. Listening to stories about family members allows us to identify predispositions related to ancestors' behaviors that may have impacted a person in both negative and positive ways.

It's interesting how people describe their ancestors' lives and legacies. The power of a person's story makes its way down through generational lines. Some people tell stories about how a person in their family line was known for their humility, kindness, generosity, wisdom, or deep faith in God. While other ancestors are remembered as being selfish, controlling, unforgiving, angry, judgmental, abusive, and distant from God.

Although every person will leave a legacy, no one can control how their story will be told, or how they will be remembered. Thankfully, while a person is still alive, they have opportunities to impact whether their legacy will include a godly heritage that future generations will desire to emulate; or a legacy that future generations will not want to emulate. But be assured, your life and legacy will influence your generational line.

Life is lived in a story

tim+anne

We were out to dinner one night with good friends. God has knit our hearts together with these people over the years, and we really enjoy being with them. Whenever we get together, conversations always include talking about our spiritual lives. We take turns sharing what God is doing in our hearts and marriage, or where we may be struggling. One evening they asked us this question, *How do you want to be remembered after you die?*

Frankly, we hadn't really thought all that much about leaving a legacy. At least, not in a way that we could clearly articulate. So, we told them we'd need some time to put our thoughts into words. The next time we met, we told them we had taken their question seriously and had spent time praying about things we really value. And we shared with them how we wanted our values to be reflected in our legacy. We said:

> *We'd like to be remembered as a man and woman who saw themselves not just as God's children, but as His beloved daughter and son. We hope we are remembered as people who were able to see others as God sees them, because we were able to see ourselves through that same lens. We hope we're remembered as a couple that never gave up on God—or others. A couple who were able to forgive because we were forgiven.*

We'd like to be remembered as a loving and faithful son/ daughter, parent, grandparent, and friend. We'd like for people to remember us as being humble, teachable, kind, and generous.

As we thought about our story, we'd like our kids, grand- kids, and ancestors to describe it as two people who fell in love, married, fully embraced God's creational mar- riage design, and became "missionaries-to-marriage." Hopefully, our passion for marriage will be imparted gen- erationally, and the fruit of what we modeled will be seen in future generations.

*We'd like to be remembered as people who began every- thing by **I.O.T.L.** (inquire of the Lord). And together—in unity—we trusted God, took risks, prayed passionate prayers, and shed godly tears. We'd like to be remem- bered as a couple who lived in The Larger Story with God as the main character. And we would love for oth- ers to tell stories that revealed God's heart through the choices we made and the ways we lived—as a couple who weren't afraid to dream BIG dreams, and who loved oth- ers WHOLEheartedly.*

How about you? Two generations from now if one of your descendants were describing you, your life, and legacy, what would they say? Maybe a better question is *What would you want them to say?* Regarding mar- riage, what kind of marriage legacy will your descendants describe about you?

ARE YOU UP FOR A REAL LIFE CHALLENGE?

Beginning today, as far as it depends on you, are you willing to passionately invest in leaving a marriage legacy that includes honoring covenant, treasuring your spouse, being forgiving and kind, and passionately embracing God's creational marriage design? If so, take some time to write it out, and then plan a date with your spouse and together review the personal legacies you want to leave. As a bonus challenge, write out what you would both like your marriage legacy to be. Our sense is this will be a SOUL*gasm* experience for you.

20 TAKEAWAYS FROM 40+ YEARS OF MARRIAGE

One of our heart's desires is that a part of our legacy relates to marriage. More than a year ago, we celebrated forty years of marriage. Looking back, the years have gone by so quickly. Throughout our marriage we've enjoyed different seasons, including early marriage years, having babies, raising a family, ongoing church involvement, and engaging in countless activities during our four children's grammar, middle, high-school, and college years. We've enjoyed sporting events, concerts, recitals, graduations, fire department promotion/retirement parties, vacations, camping trips, and family gatherings.

We've experienced the joys of children getting married. And we continue to celebrate our five amazing grandchildren. We've worshipped in different churches, changed careers a few times, and have lived in four different states (Illinois, Michigan, California, and Colorado). We've celebrated the births of family and friends' babies, visited loved ones in hospitals, set up hospice beds in our home, walked family and friends to their graves—and we've experienced innumerable SOUL*gasm* moments.

As we review decades of marriage, it's not a Facebook highlight reel. Most of our highlights are found in routine, day-to-day things. We love the *ordinary* moments spent hanging out with family, going for walks with our kids and dogs, watching a good film, and hiking in the mountains. After all these years, there is still no one we would rather spend the day with than each other. In fact, one of the best parts of our years together has been our ongoing conversations. And after much hard work, and all the ups and downs in our marriage, thankfully, we both still say *we love being married*.

Below are *20 Takeaways from 40+ Years of Marriage.* We pray these will be encouraging and challenging. You may notice that many of these are things we've already covered in Parts One and Two.

1- Being married includes having troubles. Marriage is not a fairy-tale fantasy about a never-ending honeymoon. As we've stated before, First Corinthians 7:20 says, "Those who marry will face trouble." It's true! We've experienced marital troubles—*every* couple does. The truth is we continue to experience troubles. But for us, the key is to view every trouble as an *opportunity*, rather than an *obstacle*. Troubles invite a couple to grow, to learn about God, each other, and themselves. Troubles open the door to experience SOUL*gasm* and discover a deeper level of intimacy with God and each other.

2- Grow in seeing yourself as God sees you. This challenge is not just a good idea—it's foundational for healthy relationships. The process of growing in intimacy with God teaches you how to be comfortable in your own skin and celebrate your unique design. It's a journey that's worth every step. As you realize just how much God loves you, loving yourself can become a reality. As you understand how your good Father celebrates you—just the way you are—you are able to celebrate who He made you to be, and who you are becoming. This enables you to better love and celebrate your spouse (and others). The wisest way to truly love your spouse is to begin by loving and celebrating who God made *you* to be.

3- Make the choice each day to live in the "Larger Story" where *God* is the main character; instead of living life in the "smaller story," where *self* is the main character. Remember, your story and the memories you are *building* together are created one day—one moment—at a time. Every day includes an invitation to make your marriage a priority by focusing first on God, and being other-centered and kind toward your spouse and others. But that doesn't happen by accident. Living in the Larger Story is a decision you make one moment at time.

4- Choose a lifestyle that is grounded in forgiveness. A simple two-word definition we regularly use to describe marriage is "inexhaustible forgiveness." Have you ever noticed that some of the most joy-filled people you know are those who extend grace and live out forgiveness? Remember, forgiveness begins with a decision. In marriage, this goes beyond asking your spouse to forgive you for things you did (commission); it also includes asking for forgiveness for things you failed to do (omission). Being able to say, "I'm sorry for not loving you well, for not encouraging you more, for not presupposing the best in you"—that's an advanced step in forgiveness. Our experience has taught us that the only way a person is able to forgive like this, is when they have learned how to receive forgiveness from God.

5- Understand God's design for marriage. After getting married, couples often spend their time, energy, and resources investing in things, such as careers, parenting, church, sports, the arts, hobbies, and so on. Certainly, many of these are important and can be life-enriching. However, inordinately focusing on these things can inhibit the ongoing exploration of what it means for two to "become one."[1] Learning what it means to live a Christ-centered marriage is a journey. It's not like any other relationship. Instead, it's a one-of-a-kind, one-flesh, covenant relationship where a husband and wife can live out equality, mutuality, and co-lead together. That said, no one begins a marriage automatically understanding what that means. It takes an investment of time and energy to grow, and healthy growth must be intentional.

6- Grow in understanding yourself. As we've seen in previous chapters, the Bible says, "Pay close attention to yourself and to your teaching."[2] Be willing to live with a sense of curiosity about yourself, your spouse, and your family. Proverbs 11:14 says, "In abundance of counselors there is victory." Counsel may look different for every person. Counsel can include inviting a wise person to speak into your life. That person may be a professional counselor, pastor, spiritual advisor, church small group leader, or trusted friend. Surrounding yourself with an abundance of counselors often begins by being willing to open yourself up to a third party and to their observations of your life.

As a person commits to understanding themselves and living in community, they better understand that they only "know in part."[3] This gives them the maturity to be willing to consider the possibility of seeing things in new ways. It begins with the premise that says: "I don't have all the answers." It is incredibly valuable to be willing to get curious about yourself, your spouse, your families of origin, and anything that may be *blocking* you from being all God created you to be. Being open to God's healing power can become the springboard to advancing in intimacy. For us, even after decades of marriage, we continue to invest in counseling. This helps us to stay humble as we continue to grow in learning more about God, ourselves, and each other.

7- Celebrate SPIRIT + SOUL + BODY ONENESS. First Thessalonians 5:23 says we are created with a spirit, soul, and body. In marriage, two people miraculously become one. So, that means a married couple is able to enjoy spirit, soul, and body oneness with another human being. But what does that really mean?

+ SPIRIT oneness includes being in relationship with God and understanding your true identity—that you are God's *beloved* son/daughter.

+ SOUL oneness includes growing in intimacy with your spouse. This includes advancing in what it means to know another person and be fully known by them. It includes Reflecting and Revealing God to your spouse. Throughout your marriage, as you advance in friendship and intimacy, you position yourself to experience SOUL*gasm* moments, which have a way of transforming the *ordinary* into the *extraordinary*.

+ BODY oneness includes celebrating the unique ways God designed a man and woman. After all, *God is pro-sex!* That means sex was His idea. In marriage, couples are invited to experience what it means for a husband and wife to be "naked without shame."[4]

8- When making decisions, begin everything with God, and implement the Traffic Light Principle. This is one practical tool we offer couples who are looking for ways to live together as one. How different would the outcome of a couple's decisions be if they committed to implementing the **Traffic Light Principle**? Here's how you start:

+ Begin your decision making by inviting God into your process. The Bible says, "See to it that you do not refuse Him who is speaking,"[5] and "Take captive every thought to make it obedient to Christ."[6] Listening to God is a learned behavior. We cannot overemphasize the importance of growing in your listening skills.

+ Individually ask God for wisdom. "If any of you lacks wisdom, you should ask God, who gives generously to all without finding fault, and it will be given to you."[7]

After you've asked God for wisdom, we challenge couples to wait until they *both* have "green lights" from God before pulling the trigger on decisions. In order to *build* SOUL*gasm* moments in marriage, unity with God and one another should always trump disunity. Remember, God is much more interested in husband and wife unity, than He is in either one getting their own way.

Side Note: The **Traffic Light Principle** presupposes both the husband and wife have a measure of emotional health. And that includes being humble and teachable. If either spouse chooses to intentionally respond by being controlling, demanding, discounting, or disrespectful toward their spouse, it will negatively impact potential success in this unity principle.

9- When you come to a crossroad in your life—choose the more difficult path. The more difficult path requires a deeper level of trust in God. It's a path that helps you grow in maturity, and results in increased humility. Choosing the more difficult path will leave the less difficult path for others to take. In marriage, the difficult path may be forgiving your spouse—again and again—and finding ways to speak the truth in love. It may look like serving your spouse, even if you don't think they deserve it. Choosing the more difficult path can be as simple as choosing to be patient, kind, and loving, while reflecting Jesus to them.

10- Have regular "D.O.F" days (Days-of-Fun). Christians have a tendency to take life pretty seriously. Sometimes fun is at the bottom of their priority list because it may seem to lack purpose. But you are created in the image of a God who is fun! He is the One who created people to live a balanced life that includes SOUL*gasm* moments. And more often than not, those moments come from rest. We encourage couples to purposely plan regular dates that focus on celebrating and enjoying each other. When was the last time you shared your goals, desires, and dreams for your life and marriage? Our encouragement is to always have a vision and dreams for your marriage. Remember, the Bible says, "Where there is no vision, the people perish."[8] And when you dream—dream BIG!

11- Take ownership and responsibility for your life and the pace at which you choose to live. We live with technology that provides endless ways to communicate with others. We have computers and smart phones that allow us to text, email, Facetime, and Snapchat. In fact, we have so many different ways to connect that social media can easily turn into an intimacy and SOUL*gasm blocker*.

When Psalm 46:10 (NIV) tells a person to "Be still, and know that I am God," it's not an easy task in today's world. But it is something you cannot afford to put on hold, or add to your future bucket list. Being still is a choice. It's something you can choose right now as a lifestyle. For us, God often speaks during times of rest, rather than in busyness and chaos.

Sometimes hearing God's voice is easier for those who choose to live simply. Therefore, rather than focusing on acquiring more power, a certain promotion, or material things—consider making the choice to put God, your spouse, and family at the top of your priority list. Practically speaking, think about what would have to change in your life in order for that to be a reality.

12- Live out marriage covenant. Too many Christian couples lead robotic lives, dictated by packed schedules. This results in their lives and marriage becoming *comfortably numb*. Tragically, the culture that families are currently being raised in continues to move toward a "progressive," secular, humanistic, theologically liberal relativism. This opens the door for people to easily default to worshipping at the altar of political correctness. And this includes an inordinate focus on feelings and self-determined truths, based on personal preferences. As this occurs, it becomes far too easy to lose sight of God's purpose for your life and marriage.

For example, when counseling couples, we've heard far too many husbands and wives declare that they have fallen out of love with their spouse. These declarations are followed by a decision to divorce, solely based on how a person feels, or based on the lack of feelings they are experiencing. The couple focuses on honoring their feelings, rather than honoring the covenant they made with God and their spouse. Consider this: Feeling "out of love" can be a flag that invites a person to look deeper, in order to better understand what may be missing, what needs to be restored, or healed. Feeling "out of love" can be an opportunity to include a godly, third party to help a couple navigate their way through seasons of confusion.

But far too often a husband/wife is involved with another person. In some cases, the decision to begin a new relationship is a distraction that *blocks* any opportunity for a couple to process through their pain in healthy ways. A spouse then attempts to justify their adultery by declaring they have met their soul mate, the "one" who truly understands them. But when a person enters a marriage covenant and says, "I do," the person they say those words to becomes "the one" and their soul mate—until death parts them.

13- Guard your heart. The Bible talks a lot about the heart. So much so that Proverbs 4:23 (NIV) gives a sober warning, "Above all else, guard your heart, for everything you do flows from it." When the Bible says *above all else*—that gets our attention. A person's heart is a core component of what it means to be made in the image of God.[9] The Enemy understands this, and he continually looks for ways to wound, numb, and harden a person's heart. If he can succeed at this, he can directly impact the heart of a marriage.

If we asked you to do a quick "heart check," how would you say your heart is doing? One way to know is by monitoring what comes out of your mouth. The Bible says, "The mouth speaks what the heart is full of."[10] Pause and consider what typically comes out of your mouth. Are your words positive, encouraging, and life-giving; or negative, critical, and life-draining? How you respond to this question dramatically impacts the heart of your marriage.

When we address married couples, we challenge them to guard the heart of their marriage. This includes making intentional investments in shared interests, hobbies, counseling, and soul-care activities. These are just a few examples of ways to continue growing and experiencing new things— together. If we asked you to do a quick "heart check" with regards to your marriage—what comes out of your mouth when you talk about your marriage? What condition is the heart of your marriage in right now?

14- Invest in maintaining your sense of humor. Would your spouse describe you as a person who has a sense of humor? Is it difficult for you to laugh at yourself? Because life and marriage are difficult. And without a sense of humor, it's hard to laugh at the things that can easily frustrate or trigger a person. Making an investment in maintaining your sense of humor will include managing your stress. Have you ever noticed that when people are stressed, they don't laugh very often? Our experience is that laughter can help put a problem into perspective, and with the right attitude, can even lead to experiencing SOUL*gasm*.

15- Live out unconditional love. We love this quote by Frederick Buechner, "We were made by a loving God to love one another. That other person is part of us."[11] In other words, we are built for community. We're ALL made in God's image, and connected as brothers and sisters in Christ. We define unconditional marital love as loving your spouse, without expecting anything in return. This requires each spouse to be in relationship with God, who enables them to walk out unconditional love.

16- Make humility an important life priority. "God is opposed to the proud, but gives grace to the humble."[12] Certainly, no one wants God to oppose them. Yet the truth is every person struggles with pride to various degrees. Therefore, replacing pride with humility begins by taking an honest assessment of your life, and being willing to apologize for any prideful ways. As a person matures, they let go of their need for validation from others, and they grow in seeing themselves as God sees them. As this occurs, a person is filled with a peace "which surpasses all understanding."[13]

If you asked us to name our life priorities, humility would be near the top of our list. We challenge you to look for ways every day to "clothe yourself with humility."[14] And look for ways to practice gratitude by being thankful for all God has given you. Celebrate who He says you are—your true identity—God's *beloved* son or daughter.

17- Never be ashamed of the gospel. When people become curious and ask about the *hope* they observe in your life and marriage, what would you tell them? The Bible says, "Always be prepared to give an answer to everyone who asks you to give the reason for the hope you have. But do this with gentleness and respect."[15] Are you prepared to humbly share with gentleness and respect the hope that is within you? Always remember that the gospel has power.[16] Of course, every person has a story, but we believe the story of Jesus Christ—His birth, life, death, and life-giving resurrection—is the greatest story ever told.

18- Seek first the kingdom of God. As much as we love marriage and are called to challenge people to return to God's creational marriage design, we understand that *marriage is not "it."* In *NAKED: Reclaiming Sexual Intimacy in Marriage* we write, "Don't desire marriage in such a way that you lose your contentment in—and love for—God. *Why?* Because we believe only Jesus Christ can fill the deepest longings of a person's heart."[17]

Therefore, make your top life priority to "seek first the kingdom of God."[18] Our encouragement is to arrange your life and marriage in ways that bring God glory and advance His kingdom.

19- I.O.T.L. If we wanted something etched into our tombstones, it would be "**I.O.T.L.**" We believe inviting God into your process is the wisest first step a person can take in their life, marriage, and decision-making process. The next critical step is to *listen to God*. (See Appendix D for more on this subject.) Being able to grow in your listening skills includes a disciplined commitment. How would you answer this question: *Are you a good* *listener?* We challenge you to look for ways to grow your listening skills. Without a doubt, this will have a positive impact on your intimacy with God and your spouse.

20- PRAY for your marriage. Prayer is an act of intimacy that provides supernatural power and protection. Commit to regularly praying for your spouse and with your spouse. We encourage you to regularly pray blessings over your marriage and family. And feel free to pray a blessing over us as well <smile>.

We trust the above *20 Takeaways from 40+ Years of Marriage* has encouraged and challenged you. We believe healthy, joy-filled, life-giving marriages have so much kingdom-advancing potential.

ARE YOU UP FOR A REAL LIFE CHALLENGE?

Plan a date with your spouse and review the above list. Take time to evaluate what was presented and add things that you think are important. Next, together develop a marriage plan. Remember, *fail to plan; plan to fail.* Schedule regular follow-up times to review what you are learning, and always remember to celebrate your accomplishments.

CHAPTER 15

WHAT'S THE "SECRET INGREDIENT" IN MARRIAGE?

In the previous chapter, we talked about the importance of leaving a legacy, and we offered a number of marriage takeaways. But there is one more important ingredient in a life-giving marriage.

Life is lived in a story

tim

Are you familiar with the McDonald's advertising jingle from the mid-seventies: *"Two all-beef patties, special sauce, lettuce, cheese, pickles, onions, on a sesame-seed bun"*? When this triple-decker sandwich was introduced, all of those ingredients were familiar—except for the *special* sauce. People wondered: *What were the secret ingredients that made the special sauce so special?* Sometimes marriage can feel that way, especially during difficult seasons. A person may wonder: *What am I missing? What's the recipe for the mysterious, marriage special sauce?*

Recently, I've asked a number of married women and men this question: *What do you think is the secret ingredient in a successful marriage?* Their responses varied. Here are just a few: "Being able to forgive, being strong communicators, humility, prayer, understanding the importance of unity, being willing to be vulnerable, continuing to pursue each other, enjoying a good sex life, having a sense of humor by not taking yourself too seriously, being financially secure, presupposing the best in each other, and keeping our life priorities in order."

Anne and I agree with all these responses, and every one of these ingredients are SOUL*gasm builders*.

However, for me personally, I believe the "secret sauce" in marriage is PASSION. My real-life experience is that people who are passionate about God and marriage are life-giving. They have an amazing ability to breathe life into those around them. Passionate husbands and wives impact marriage in positive ways. And they have an ability to transform *ordinary* moments into SOUL*gasm* experiences.

How about you, what are you passionate about? I've heard men enthusiastically describe their favorite sports team or hobby, their strategy for lowering their golf score, landing the big fish, or accomplishing their next personal goal. I've heard women eagerly describe their latest adventure, new risks they are taking, battles they are engaging in, or new insights and revelations they are experiencing. These are all good things. But I rarely hear husbands and wives describe their marriage in passionate ways. It would be so great to hear more people enthusiastically talking about marriage, advancing in intimacy, and experiencing SOUL*gasm*.

Successfully advancing in intimacy involves being passionate about God and your spouse, and this often leads to experiencing SOUL*gasm*. A good place to begin your journey toward increased intimacy includes identifying some of the *blocks* that may be in place for you. God longs for people to advance in intimacy and live with passion, and this includes trusting Him and taking risks.

Practically speaking, pay attention to negative internal messages or damaging self-talk that keeps you from moving forward. Identify any fears you may have about intimacy and living with passion. Some spouses are afraid of failure or being rejected. The remedy to fear is living out your true identity, and trusting that God is good and He has your back.

As you process advancing in intimacy and growing in passion, I encourage you to begin with a season of prayerful introspection. For some, including a mentor, counselor, or spiritual director may help you identify any lies you believe about God or yourself. Once you've identified any lies, replace those ungodly beliefs with truths. Regularly practice speaking God's truths over yourself. This helps a person to live out their true identity, which is foundational to advancing in intimacy and living a life of passion.

Spouses may be wondering: *How can I increase passion in my marriage?* For me, maintaining passion in practical ways includes staying in my own lane; not trying to micromanage Anne or others; being willing to recognize areas of immaturity, and then taking ownership and responsibility for my part in our marriage—as I commit to growing up.

THE VICTIM MENTALITY

One area that regularly surfaces in the counseling office is the *victim mentality*. When a person is struggling, they tend to use statements that result in them being the victim. For example, *If* (fill in the blank) *then* (fill in the blank). *If* my husband were more expressive, *then* I could engage him. *If* my wife were less of a perfectionist, *then* I could have more freedom to relax.

We encourage husbands and wives to begin a conversation by starting out with an "I" statement. For example, *I* choose to resist living in the smaller story where *it's all about me.* And instead, *I* will choose to live in the Larger Story where *it's not about me.* Therefore, *I* will work on areas that are my responsibility, and release control of areas that are my spouse's responsibility. *I* will choose to please God first, and focus on *my* behavior, rather than inordinately focusing on what *I* think *my spouse* needs to do.

We encourage husbands/wives to invite God to give you the desire and ability to increase passion in your heart. A wise first step is to **I.O.T.L.**—and ask your good Father to lead and guide you in revealing passion to your spouse. Remember, God has wisdom and passion-increasing ideas a person could never think of on their own.

What might that look like for you? It can be helpful to invest in better understanding yourself (and your spouse's) family of origin, temperament, love language, and specific things that are life-giving to them. For Anne and me, celebrating life with family and friends, hiking in the mountains, making our sexual intimacy a priority, enjoying a good meal, watching a great film, and engaging in *ordinary* and *extraordinary* things we love to do *together*, helps rekindle passion.

Another great place for Anne and me to rekindle passion is to spend time with our kids and grandkids. Just being with them, sharing *ordinary* and *extraordinary* moments, refuels our passion. Remember, it's not how passionate you think you are, but how you are engaging passionately with others, and how they are responding. The following quote by an unknown author describes passion in marriage and touches on the amazing uniqueness in intimacy, unity, and SOUL*gasm*: "There shall be such oneness between you that when one weeps, the other shall taste salt."

Before moving on, how about you? What do you consider the "secret sauce" in your marriage?

A RECIPE FOR SUCCESS

Throughout our authors/reader journey, we have said that "Every marriage will experience troubles."[1] The reality is that marriage was never meant to be a fairy-tale fantasy about a never-ending honeymoon. Our experience has taught us that having troubles is not *bad* news, it's actually *good* news. This passage can be an encouragement because it reminds a spouse that you are not alone, and every husband and wife struggle to varying degrees. Just knowing that troubles are a shared experience can often normalize the rough patches.

While we understand that every couple's struggles are different and each person is unique, there are common ingredients that seem to run through couples' stories that we'd like to address in this closing chapter. It's been our experience that the majority of problems clients share with us often involve immaturity. Without minimizing a person's struggle, we recognize the damage immaturity can cause in relationships, and the ways immaturity relates to selfishness, which can *block* couples from experiencing SOUL*gasm* moments.

We understand that when a person first decides to make an appointment to see a counselor, pastor, or spiritual director, they are committing to submit themselves to a third party. It signifies they are ready to take a next step, trust God, and take a closer look at their life and marriage. They are intentionally inviting someone else to help them identify destructive patterns. While negative patterns can be as unique as the person, immaturity and selfishness are almost always part of the problem.

Pause and take a moment to consider negative behaviors in your own life. The list may include negative responses, such as avoidance, procrastination, control, rebellion, or outbursts of anger. Whatever their name, they are often childish and selfish responses rather than adult responses. Sometimes, just calling the immature behavior what it is becomes a part of the recipe for success that enables a person to take next steps toward positive change.

When we recognize areas of immaturity, we often share a favorite Bible passage. It says, "When I was a child, I talked like a child, I thought like a child, I reasoned like a child. When I became a man, I put the ways of childhood behind me."[2] Sometimes we gently ask the person, "Are there any ways that your marriage struggle can be connected to your need to put away childish things and focus on growing up?" And sometimes we challenge husbands/wives in a more direct way by suggesting to them that "It's time to grow up."

GROW UP!

Life is lived in a story

anne

Tim and I are gifted very differently. These differences work well together in the counseling office. If you were to observe our sessions, you would see that Tim is gifted with leadership, encouragement, and faith. Tim is a good listener. He is able to lead people through their struggles by encouraging them, speaking godly truth to them, and having faith that God can heal.

As I've observed him over the years, I am continually amazed by how direct he can be with clients. I believe one of the reasons why he can speak so candidly to them is because he truly loves people. He believes with his whole heart that every person matters to God. It's a depth of love people immediately sense, and this allows Tim to be very straightforward. Instead of clients feeling shamed by his direct style, they feel understood and loved. I can recall countless times when God used Tim to shine light into a dark place as he encouraged the person to take a next step toward health and wholeness.

For example, at a Marriage Advance years ago, a man spoke to us during the break about his marriage struggles. We suggested he make an appointment, and he confidently responded that he "would think about it." He added, "I was in the military, and the only reason I came to this workshop was because I heard that Tim was a retired fire chief, and I thought his paramilitary background made him somewhat credible to me."

When he and his wife arrived at the office for their first appointment, we were immediately reminded of this man's strong personality. It was easy to understand how his style of relating could be intimidating to those around him, especially his wife. During the initial session, we learned that the husband had grown up without a strong father figure. He described his dad as an alcoholic and his mom as passive and distant. He had to learn to negotiate life on his own. So, he adopted a lot of controlling and negative behaviors that helped him survive. The problem was, those negative behaviors may have helped him survive his childhood, but they were not working well for him when it came to *building* intimacy with his spouse.

Whenever I asked him a question, he was quick to blame someone. In spite of the confidence he worked so hard to project, he seemed to be afraid, and conveyed a victim mentality. Nothing was his fault. His struggles and problems were all about his wife, boss, friends, church leaders, and so on.

After listening for a while longer, Tim responded, "You've described the ways your problems are everyone else's fault. But what part of your marriage struggles do *you* take ownership and responsibility for?"

That question changed the atmosphere in our office and opened the door for a deeper conversation. The man's failure to take ownership and responsibility for his life had damaging effects to his marriage and other relationships.

As our session came to a close, Tim leaned forward, looked the husband directly in his eyes, and said, "Before we close in prayer, I want to say something that might be a little difficult for you to hear right now, but if you listen closely, I believe that it may help you tremendously."

Again, the husband seemed a bit uncertain of what was coming next, but he was willing to listen. He responded, "Give me your bottom line, Tim."

Tim said, "My bottom line for you is simply this, 'It's time for you to quit blaming your bride and others—and *grow up!*'"

There are times when a client needs a strong challenge. And although my counseling style is much different than Tim's, we both agree that many roots of immaturity *block* intimacy. Being lovingly challenged to take ownership and responsibility to *grow up* is often hard to hear, but if well received, it can be life changing.

Of course, a simple *"Grow up"* is not the solution to every marriage problem. Exploring family-of-origin behaviors and propensities, dealing with wounds, and working through forgiveness issues are all part of a person's healing process. But a key next step for every husband/wife is to take ownership and responsibility to advance in personal maturity, soul care, and spiritual formation. Couples who are willing to take these steps are better equipped to work through marriage struggles. And this results in greater intimacy with God and their spouse, and it positions them to experience more SOUL*gasm* moments.

Can we ask, *What areas in your life do you need to grow up and take ownership and responsibility for?* We challenge you to **I.O.T.L.** and ask God for specific next steps. Write down anything you sense. Then make a plan—*fail to play; plan to fail*. Remember, a plan begins with a first step, then a second, and a third. Write out your steps and ask a few people to keep you accountable. Then trust God, take a risk, watch and pray, and monitor how intimacy and SOUL*gasms* increase in your life—and marriage.

EPILOGUE

THE FIX IS IN

Life is lived in a story

tim

Early in my firefighting career, I recall a heart attack emergency call. The paramedics arrived and a man was slumped over the steering wheel. He had no pulse and no respirations—in layman's terms, he was *dead-as-a-doornail.*

The highly trained paramedics went to work. They quickly extricated the man from the vehicle, initiated CPR, started an IV, administered drugs, defibrillated him a number of times, and in a matter of a few intense minutes, his heart began to beat—*he was alive!* They placed the patient on a stretcher, and then headed to the hospital lights-and-sirens, pedal-to-the-metal fast; and as the ambulance was arriving at the emergency room, the man was actually talking to them!

After the paramedics did their paper work and restocked supplies, before heading back to the firehouse, they checked in to see how the patient was doing. Thankfully, he was doing well. He caught the paramedics' eyes and waved at them to come closer to him. He gently whispered, "*Thank you for saving my life. Just before the accident, I was on my way to the race track to place a bet.*" The man looked around to see if anyone was listening; he leaned in and whispered, "If you want to bet on a winning horse today, put your money on *Perplexed* in the sixth race." Looking around once again he added, "*The fix is in!*"

As it turned out, that day at the local race track the winner of the sixth race was a horse named *Perplexed*. He was right—*the fix was in*. As a side note, I can neither confirm nor deny if anyone at the firehouse placed a bet on *Perplexed*. But I seem to recall lots of firefighters leaving the station the next morning with BIG smiles on their faces!

THE "FIX IS IN" REGARDING MARRIAGE

Just like the race where *Perplexed* was set up to win, we believe *"the fix is in"* regarding marriage. The end of the story has already been written. God is going to return one day and restore all things as they were originally designed—and this includes His creational marriage design. Until that epic day, we believe that in God's power, husbands and wives can return to the mutuality and functional authority principles of Paradise.

We've already stated that *God is good*. We want to offer another bedrock truth: *God is love*. The Bible brings good news, saying, "For I am convinced that neither death, nor life, nor angels, nor principalities, nor things present, nor things to come, nor powers, nor height, nor depth, nor any other created thing, will be able to separate us from the love of God, which is in Christ Jesus our Lord."[1] The essence of marriage is love, and as a person focuses on being unconditionally loved by God, it becomes the pathway to unconditionally loving a spouse—and others.

It makes us wonder: *Might this be a* Kairos *time*—the right, critical, opportune moment—*for Christians to humble themselves, repent, and return to God's creational marriage principles?* As this occurs, healthy marriages and unity in the church will attract those outside the church as they are supernaturally drawn to explore the unity, oneness, and intimacy modeled in churches, Christian communities of faith, and Christ-centered marriages.

And this will open doors to share about the birth + life + death + life-giving resurrection of Jesus Christ. In what many people consider the most famous passage in the Bible, it describes the simple gospel message in one sentence, saying, "For God so loved the world, that He gave His only begotten Son; that whoever believes in Him shall not perish, but have eternal life."[2]

WE HAVE A DREAM

The Bible says, "Where there is no vision, the people perish."[3] We have a number of dreams surrounding marriage:

+ *We have a dream* that Christian husbands and wives will give 100 percent to passionately living out God's "two become one" and "naked without shame" creational marriage design. This will include advancing in intimacy, SOUL*gasm* experiences, and celebrating *ordinary* and *extraordinary* moments in life—and marriage.

+ *We have a dream* where we envision Christian couples embracing mutual equality—*both* man and woman made in the image of God. And *together*, couples exercising functional authority—both the husband and wife living out the procreation and dominion (rulership) mandates.[4]

+ *We have a dream* for married couples to do great things. Throughout a number of decades, we've meditated on John 14:12 (NIV) that says, "Very truly I tell you, whoever believes in me will do the works I have been doing, and *they will do even greater things* than these, because I am going to the Father." Unfortunately, this passage does not spell out what the "greater things" are.

For years we thought *greater things* included miracles, healings, demonic deliverance, people raised from the dead, and the evangelization of nations. However, as we've continued to meditate on this passage, we wonder if *greater things* include reclaiming God's creational marriage principles, fiercely fighting for marriages and families, and passionately embracing mutuality and functional equality—which will result in seeing God's glory in couples' marriage stories.

Do you remember a New Testament couple named Priscilla and Aquila? They were married and ministered *together*. The Bible talks about an interaction between Priscilla, Aquila, and Apollos, who the Bible described as an eloquent speaker. The text reads, "He [Apollos] began to speak out boldly in the synagogue. But when Priscilla and Aquila heard him, they took him aside and explained to him the way of God more accurately."[5]

Similar to Priscilla and Aquila, we believe part of our calling is to explain *God's creational marriage way more accurately*. This includes a man and woman, "becoming one"[6] and celebrating being "naked without shame."[7]

Throughout the years, we've been asked, "Can you explain your motivation to invest your lives sharing about marriage?"—that's a good question.

Reviewing our primary motivations regarding why we are so passionate about God's creational marriage design, two of them include the following:

> 1. PEOPLE MATTER TO GOD.
> 2. MARRIAGE MATTERS TO GOD.

We are truly hopeful for marriage. *Why?* Because our *hope* is based on the "living *hope* through the resurrection of Jesus Christ"[8]—*to God be the glory.*

OUR PRIMARY MESSAGE

We want to finish this book in the same way that we conclude our REAL LIFE advances and workshops. We say, "As much as we love marriage—our primary message is *not* about marriage, but about the *Maker* of marriage—God the Father + Son + Holy Spirit."

The Bible emphasizes the importance to "build up the church."[9] We believe there is untapped, building-up-the-church potential in God's creational marriage design—a man and woman "becoming one,"[10] "co-leading + co-serving + co-equals in Christ,"[11] and celebrating being "naked without shame."[12]

LOVE and **MARRIAGE** ... can you think of any other words that have such life-giving potential?

May the God who is both great and good
make your marriage stronger and your hearts braver.
May He create not only a willingness to die for your
marriage but also a passion to live for it.

APPENDIX A

CO-LEADERSHIP IN MARRAIGE

In *TOGETHER: Reclaiming Co-Leadership in Marriage*,[1] we write about how God's plurality and nature relate to His original design and purposes for marriage. In *TOGETHER*, we unpack the functional equality and mutual authority—what we refer to as *co-leadership*—that the first husband and wife enjoyed before sin entered the marriage story. We ask, *Why did God create marriage?* We believe God created marriage to tell a story.

In the beginning, man and woman were both created in God's image and likeness.[2] That said, it's important to remember that humans who are made in the image and likeness of God can never fully Reflect and Reveal God's essence, because men and women are humans—and God is God. Nevertheless, before sin entered the story, the man and woman were intrinsically equal.

In the beginning, man and woman were both commanded to carry out God's mandates. They were both given the procreation mandate to be fruitful and multiply, and they were both given the dominion (rulership) mandate.[3] As co-leaders, the husband and wife ruled over the fish, birds, animals, and so on. *Together*, the husband and wife enjoyed mutuality and shared authority. Before sin entered the story, the man and woman were functionally equal.

In the beginning, before sin entered the story, there was no patriarchy, headship, hierarchy, female subordination, or the husband designated as the wife's leader, authority, or "spiritual cover."

Tragically, co-leading in mutuality was lost when the woman and man sinned. Some of the results included male rulership, hierarchy, patriarchy, headship, female subordination, and complementarian marriage views. All of these marriage views came *after* sin. They did not reflect the functional equality and mutual authority—co-leadership—in God's creational marriage design.

Let's briefly review different marriage views:

+ In the male rulership marriage view,[4] *gender trumps*.
+ In the hierarchical/traditional/complementarian marriage views, *gender trumps*.
+ In the egalitarian marriage view as we currently understand it, functional equality and mutuality are highly valued. Dr. Gilbert Bilezikian, a long-time proponent of egalitarian theology, offers ten alternatives for reaching "resolution of the decision-making impasses that occur when opinions differ." Including "defer to each other … exercise spiritual gifts … compromise … pray for guidance … whenever a decision affects one spouse more than the other, the spouse who has more at stake in the decision should have more say in the process … initiate joint research projects on the debated issue … decide to defer the matter to a trusted and objective

third party after agreeing to abide by his or her determination (1 Corinthians 6:5); engage in parts reversals."[5]
In the egalitarian marriage view, *individual gifts and a
pre-agreed-upon process trump.*

+ God's original marriage design (what we call *co-
leadership*) is similar to the egalitarian marriage view
because functional equality and mutuality are highly
valued. However, a couple's primary focus is including
God in the decision-making process. They both **I.O.T.L.**,
implement the **Traffic Light Principle**, and wait for
"green lights" from the Lord before making decisions.
In co-leadership, *God trumps.*

Thankfully, in the fullness of time, Jesus Christ took on human form and
came to earth. One of the amazing things Jesus did was come "to seek
and to save *that* which was lost."[6] Empowered by the Holy Spirit, Jesus
engaged the Enemy and took back *that* which was lost. We believe this
included the mutuality and functional equality in God's creational marriage design.

Jesus' birth, life, death, and life-giving resurrection opened the door for
married couples to return to the marriage principles of Paradise and
reclaim God's creational marriage design. The good news is that couples
can once again co-lead together—*naked without shame*—as they *become
one* and celebrate spirit, soul (SOUL*gasm*), and body oneness. Having
walked out co-leadership for over forty years, our humble opinion is that
husbands and wives don't *have to* walk out co-leadership—they *get to*.
That said, it's important to remember that our view of marriage—like all
marriage positions—is a *preference* not an *absolute*.

APPENDIX B

I.O.T.L.—INQUIRE OF THE LORD

I.O.T.L. is a simple four-letter acronym that stands for "Inquire of the Lord." **I.O.T.L.** is about seeking the presence of God. In the New Testament, the apostle Paul emphasized the importance of "taking every thought captive to Christ."[1] And throughout the Old Testament, when leaders "inquired of the Lord," they experienced victories.[2]

If you are a follower of Jesus Christ, the Holy Spirit dwells in you.[3] Therefore, it is wise to "take captive every thought to make it obedient to Christ"[4] and include Him in everything. Including God provides power and protection.

+ **I.O.T.L.** is a reminder to invite God into your life, marriage, and the decisions you make.
+ **I.O.T.L.** includes putting God first, trusting Him,[5] and asking for wisdom.[6]
+ **I.O.T.L.** will provide you with insight that no authors, teachers, or pastor/priest can provide.

Remember, **I.O.T.L.** is *not* a religious exercise. It involves a person relating to God. Picture a child saying to a good mommy/daddy, *I trust you.*

Please give me wisdom and help me to make good decisions. Similar to co-leading together, **I.O.T.L.** and including God in our decision-making process is not something we *have* to do, instead it's something we *get* to do.

APPENDIX C

THE TRAFFIC LIGHT PRINCIPLE

The **Traffic Light Principle** is about seeking the presence of God. Implementing the **Traffic Light Principle** involves putting God first, trusting Him,[1] and asking for wisdom.[2] Our real-life experience has taught us that purposefully including God in our decision-making process provides us with power, protection, and opportunities to experience SOUL*gasm*.

HOW DOES THE **TRAFFIC LIGHT PRINCIPLE** WORK?

> **Step 1**: A husband and wife individually **I.O.T.L.** (*Inquire of the Lord*). They invite God into their decision-making process and seek His wisdom. The Bible says, "If any of you lacks wisdom, you should ask God, who gives generously to all without finding fault, and it will be given to you."[3]

> **Step 2**: The second step involves couples sharing what they sense the Lord may be saying. Figuratively speaking, are they sensing a: "green light" (*go*); a "yellow light" (*slow*); or a "red light" (*no*)?

Step 3: Couples wait until they *both* have "green lights" from God—then they pull the trigger on the decision.

In addition, we encourage couples to agree on the following principles:

1. Proceed only if you are in unity. If you do not *both* have "green lights" from the Lord, agree to wait because unity with God and each other should trump disunity.

2. If your lights remain different while you are waiting, continue to pray and listen. The Bible says, "See to it that you do not refuse Him who is speaking."[4] If appropriate, include a third party for insight and wisdom. "Where there is no guidance the people fall, but in abundance of counselors there is victory."[5] Keep revisiting your decision until you sense God giving you *both* "green lights."

3. As you continue to process, it is important to understand the key component in the **Traffic Light Principle**: It includes three lights. The middle light represents God, one light represents what the wife senses from God, and one light represents what the husband senses from God.

Following are questions couples often ask about the **Traffic Light Principle**:

+ *Is a couple's main goal to be in agreement?*

No, remember Adam and Eve were in agreement when they ate the forbidden fruit—and we all know how that played out. Had either Eve or Adam asked God for a light, it would have been bright red. Therefore, a couple's agreement must be based on what they *both* sense the Lord saying.

+ *With all the time it takes to implement the* Traffic Light Principle, *taking time necessary to* I.O.T.L. *and to pray and process, how do you ever get around to making decisions?*

Early in our marriage, one of us would try to "work it" to get what they wanted, even if we did not have unity. This resulted in the decision often ending in a disaster. Implementing the **Traffic Light Principle**, even if it means slowing your decision-making process down, encourages couples to include God.

+ *Do you use the* Traffic Light Principle *on every decision?*

That is a good question; for example, we do not call our spouse from the grocery store and ask, "Do you have a green light on Granny Smith or Honeycrisp apples?" God created men and women as volitional human beings who have been given the ability to make choices. Therefore, couples can choose to ask God and include Him on decisions or not—the choice is up to them.

The Bible says, "You do not have because you do not ask."[6] It also says, "If you want favor with both God and man, and a reputation for good judgment and common sense, then trust the Lord completely; don't ever trust yourself. In *everything* you do, put God first, and *he will direct you* and crown your efforts with success."[7] The bottom line is that couples don't *have* to include God and walk together in unity—they *get* to.

+ *Marriage has so much untapped, kingdom-advancing potential. Why?*

There is power and protection in covenant—in "two becoming one."[8] Walking in unity opens the door for couples to fully celebrate being "naked without shame."[9] Furthermore, living out God's creational marriage design—as co-leaders, functional equals, and reciprocal servants—provides amazing opportunities to share with others about GOD—the Maker of marriage.

Having lived out the **Traffic Light Principle** for decades, there is one essential ingredient we've found to successfully implementing it. **This principle presupposes the husband and wife have a measure of emotional health, humility, and tender-teachable hearts**. If either spouse is controlling, demanding, discounting, or disrespectful toward their spouse, it will minimize experiencing success in this unity principle. For example, after teaching about the **Traffic Light Principle**, one husband said, "So, if I tell my wife I have a yellow or red light, then she can't do what she wants—right?"

Sadly, this husband missed the entire point of this principle. After engaging with this husband, it became apparent that he never included God, and his red or yellow light was a way to attempt to gain control, get his own way, or keep his wife from doing something she sensed the Lord saying. If either spouse defaults to control, disunity, or disagreement, and lives in the smaller story where *self* is the main character (instead of living in the Larger Story where *God* is the main character), the blessings this principle provides will be derailed. That said, if a couple reaches a log-jam, we strongly encourage them to invite a mature third party to help process making decisions.

We've experienced the blessings and benefits of including God and making decisions when we *both* have green lights from the Lord. And we would never revert to one of us having the final say, the husband having a gender trump card, or basing our decisions solely on individual gifts.

As we look back over four decades of marriage, implementing the **Traffic Light Principle** has resulted in increased intimacy with God and each other; as *together*, we've advanced in spirit + soul + body oneness.

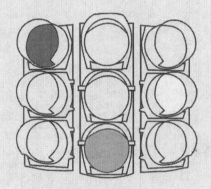

APPENDIX D

LISTENING TO GOD

Listening to God is one of the most important things a Christ-follower can do. The Bible says, "See to it that you do not refuse Him who is speaking."[1] Following are questions that are listed in our book *TOGETHER: Reclaiming Co-Leadership in Marriage*[2] to help a person's (and couple's) decision-making process:

1. Have you prayed about what you are considering?

> "Be anxious for nothing, but in everything by prayer and supplication with thanksgiving let your requests be known to God."[3]
> "Take every thought captive to Christ."[4]

2. Is what you are considering consistent with the principles in the Bible?

> "He who is spiritual appraises all things."[5]
> "If any of you lacks wisdom, let him ask of God, who gives to all generously and without reproach."[6]

3. Is what you are considering affirmed by other godly people?

"Where there is no guidance [revelation] the people fall. But in abundance of counselors there is victory."[7]

4. Will what you are considering bring glory to God?

"Whatever you do in word and deed, do all in the name of the Lord Jesus."[8]

5. Will what you are considering positively impact God's kingdom?

"Seek first His kingdom and His righteousness."[9]

Remember, the kingdom of God has one King (and the King is not the husband).

6. How does what you are considering relate to God's will for your life?

"Rejoice always; pray without ceasing; in everything give thanks; for this is God's will for you in Christ Jesus."[10]

7. Do you have peace about what you are considering?

"And the peace of God, which surpasses all understanding, will guard your hearts and your minds in Christ Jesus."[11]

8. Do you have unity with your spouse?

God's original design for marriage included mutual equality and mutual authority—what we call co-leadership.[12]

9. Will what you are considering cost you something?

"And He said to them, 'Truly I say to you, there is no one who has left house or wife or brothers or parents or children, for the sake of the kingdom of God, who will not receive many times as much at this time and in the age to come, eternal life.'"[13] Remember—cost is not always money; it often involves servanthood, sacrifice, humility, and taking the road less traveled.

10. Does what you are considering agree with your life calling and mission?

"I therefore ... urge you to walk in a manner worthy of the calling to which you have been called."[14]

"Who has saved us and called us with a holy calling, not according to our works, but according to His own purpose and grace which was granted us in Christ Jesus."[15]

11. Does what you are considering come from a pure heart?

"The LORD does not look at the things people look at. People look at the outward appearance, but the Lord looks at the heart."[16]

We are never to judge another person's heart. Nevertheless, the Bible says, "[The] mouth speaks from that which fills [the] heart."[17]

12. Does what you are considering come from a place of love?

"'YOU SHALL LOVE THE LORD YOUR GOD WITH ALL YOUR HEART, AND WITH ALL YOUR SOUL, AND WITH ALL YOUR MIND.' This is the great and foremost commandment. The second is like it, 'YOU SHALL LOVE YOUR NEIGHBOR AS YOURSELF.' On these two commandments depend the whole Law and the Prophets.'"[18]

The older we get, the more we believe that love is the ball game. The most mature followers of Christ we have known throughout our lives have been the most loving people we know.

This non-exhaustive list is not based on gender. Notice that each step equally impacts both men and women. Again, in marriage, three keys to co-leading together and making godly decisions are:

1. **I.O.T.L.** *(Inquire of the Lord)*.
2. Maximize both the husband's and wife's gifts.
3. Wait for unity (until you both have "green lights" from the Lord).

APPENDIX E

CORE REAL LIFE VALUES

Following are core REAL LIFE values[1]:

CORE TRUE IDENTITY

Individuals who understand their true identity—that they are a *beloved* son or daughter made in the image of an amazing God—are people who understand the importance of seeing themselves as their good Father God sees them. We believe a person's true identity as a human being relates to his or her sexual identity. Review the Creation account; God first created humankind in His image.[2] Keep in mind, the first human (Adam) also contained the DNA of the first woman (Eve). After creating humankind, the text goes on to describe that God created them male and female.[3]

Undeniably, men and women are different. We recognize and celebrate both masculine and feminine characteristics. We believe differences can become opportunities to Reflect and Reveal different aspects in our triune God. On the other hand, men and women are more similar—as human beings—than they are different as males and females. That said, it is important to realize that God is not a man.[4] God's essence transcends gender and sexuality.

MARITAL "ONENESS"

There is so much power and protection in marital oneness—in "two becoming one." Every person has a *spirit*, *soul*, and *body*.[5]

God's creational marriage design included:

+ **SPIRIT Oneness**—the husband and wife lived in relationship with God. As human beings made in God's image, individually and together, they Reflected and Revealed God's character to each other and to the world around them.
+ **SOUL Oneness**—the husband and wife were given dominion over every living thing.[6] They co-led in shared authority, unity, and friendship. Advancing in soul oneness involves advancing in emotional intimacy and includes experiencing SOUL*gasm*.
+ **BODY Oneness**—the husband and wife enjoyed the sexual dimension God designed for marriage.

Keep in mind, each characteristic of marital oneness—spirit, soul, body—is an invitation for a couple to *become one* and celebrate being *naked without shame*. In our experience, people often approach the mission of marriage from a perspective of outcome: things a person or couple plans to do or achieve. However, the redemptive mission in marriage is not limited to outcome but includes relationship.

GOD'S MISSION FOR MARRIAGE

Stop for a moment and ask yourself this question: *What is God's purpose—His mission—for marriage?* We use a simple Four-R alliteration to describe marriage before sin entered the story. Every husband and wife can choose to return to the principles of Paradise as they enter into covenant with God and each other. In marriage they can:

+ Reflect and Reveal: God's plurality and nature. However, it's important to remember that humans, who are made in the image and likeness of God,[7] can never fully Reflect and Reveal God's essence because men and women are humans—and God is God.
+ Rule: co-lead *together*; mutual authority; *both* are given the dominion (rulership) mandate.
+ Reproduce: commit to being fruitful and multiply; *both* the woman and man are given the procreation mandate.[8] Remember, reproducing includes having biological children, adoption, foster parenting, and spiritual parenting.

LARGER STORY VS. SMALLER STORY

We believe life can be lived in one of two stories—the Larger Story or the smaller story.[9] The way to determine which story you are living in is to ask yourself a simple question: *Who is the main character in my life story?*

If the main character in your life story is *self*, you are living in the smaller story. If the main character in your life story is *God*, you are living in the Larger Story. Living marriage in the smaller story results in a husband or wife making marriage "all about me." Living marriage in the Larger Story results in a husband and wife making their marriage "not about me." Practically speaking, the Larger Story means including God in everything, individually and together as a couple, as you make it a top priority to **I.O.T.L.**

ACKNOWLEDGMENTS

Life is lived in a story ... and writing this book has been a story filled with family and friends. Our experience is that anything successful in life involves a team. God built an amazing team for this project. The reality is there are too many team members to list. Nevertheless, we want to extend our heartfelt thanks to the following people:

+ To our Prayer Shield Team who pray for us, our marriage, family, ministry, teaching and writing. We treasure your prayers and encouragement.

+ To our parents, Jack and Pat O'Shaughnessy and Bill and Jeanne Evans, for laying a strong foundation that continues to be built on.

+ To our children: Tim, Amy and Curt, Colleen and Johnny, and Cate and Darren. *Thank you* for being willing to follow God—even when it cost you something. And to our grandchildren: Joel, Trey, Grace, Emma, Jack ... and future grandkids (& great-grandkids). Your existence brings us indescribable joy!

+ To our spiritual parents: Dr. Gilbert Bilezikian, Dick and Alice Swetman, Peter and Doris Wagner, and Chester and Betsy Kylstra. Thank you to *all* the mentors God has blessed us with over the years; the list is too long to type.

+ To our amazing REAL LIFE friends and partners: Jim and Kathy Kubik, Keith and Robyn Brodie, TJ and Deb Bratt, Adam and Jill Carter, Laurence and Jessica Coppedge, George and Melodee Cook, Daniel and Jackie Hathaway, Jason and Keeley Cormier, Bill and Barb Vroon, Chuck and Bev Osterink, Steve and Pam DeBoer, Tom and Julie Vroon, Doug and Nicole LaCroix, Danny and Angela Gieck, David and Kate Kubik, Paul and Barb Osburn, Kate and Troy DeWys, Justin Ensor, and many others. Our gratitude for your ongoing prayers, partnership, and belief in us is difficult to put into words—*thank you.*

+ To: Brandy Bruce and Marianne Hering for editing; Susan Murdock (and Michael) for interior layout and text pour in; Susan Murdock, Beryl Glass, Amy DeBoer, and Kathleen White for our cover design and illustration; and Sara Martin for the picture. You *all* became key partners in the completion of this project.

+ While writing this book, we were blessed to be on the receiving end of encouraging words and timely support that cheered us on. To Ken Gire, Brad Herman, and John Blase for your ongoing encouragement to keep writing. Special thanks to: Linda Laird, Jack and Becky Sytsema, Mary and Mike Banas, Jodi and Miles Anderson, Doug and Kate Vandenhoeck, Zach and Jordyn Osburn, Stephanie and Jay Frankhouse, John Tekautz, Tom and Jan Murray, Marty and Marilyn O'Connor, Linda and Eric Sloan, Charles and Judy Cash, Dan and Jane Evans, Anne and Mike Risher, John and Caryl O'Shaughnessy, Mike Ruman, Tom Stella ... *and so many others. Thank you* for your prayers, notes, calls, feedback, and gestures of kindness that arrived at the perfect times.

+ Thank you to Dr. Gilbert Bilezikian for writing the book foreword, and to those who endorsed our book: Dr. Mimi Haddad, Debra Fileta, Jack and

Terri Brown, Rev. Sue Bailey, Jacob and Hannah Oulette, and Dr. Wilmer Villacorta.

+ A special thank you to those who are represented (anonymously) through the stories in this book; and to the men and women in our co-leadership marriage community groups throughout the decades. Your lives tell stories that points us to God. Thank you for having the courage to share the joys and struggles of your journey. Seeing you advance in intimacy with God and each other inspires us to keep trusting God—and taking risks.

+ We thank God for and we bless others who will build on what we have written about God's creational marriage design, SOUL*gasm*, and co-leadership in marriage. Our prayer is that God builds a network of relationships united in heart about a marriage mission that matters.

+ Lastly, we thank God for creating marriage. It's our prayer that Your creational marriage design is passionately reclaimed and humbly restored.

ABOUT THE AUTHORS

photo by Sara Martin

Anne + Tim Evans have been married more than forty years and have counseled couples for decades. They are both ordained ministers, and each has master and doctor of practical ministry diplomas from Wagner Leadership Institute. They are parents, grandparents, spiritual parents, authors, and pastoral counselors. Tim is a retired fire chief; Anne is a licensed nurse and certified life-purpose coach. They live in Colorado and *together* co-lead REAL LIFE Ministries. (www.TimPlusAnne.com)

REAL LIFE MINISTRIES

REAL LIFE Ministries' mission is to help men, women, and couples advance in passionately loving God, loving a spouse, and loving others (Matthew 22:37-40). The *why* that drives REAL LIFE is **Marriage Transformation**.

REAL LIFE offers:

+ Pastoral counseling
+ Marriage tune-ups
+ Marriage intensives
+ REAL LIFE Marriage Advance seminars
+ Seven Keys to Advancing in Intimacy with Your Spouse workshops
+ Forgiveness workshops
+ Communication workshops
+ *NAKED: Reclaiming Sexual Intimacy in Marriage* workshop
+ *TOGETHER: Reclaiming Co-Leadership in Marriage* workshop
+ SOUL*gasm: Caring for Your Soul and the Soul of Your Marriage* workshop
+ Overcoming Destructive Cycles workshops
+ Premarital counseling
+ Restoring the Foundations (inner healing ministry)
+ Men's and women's gatherings

tim+anne evans

REAL LIFE ministries
www.TimPlusAnne.com
PO Box 6800
Colorado Springs, CO 80934

NOTES

Notes to the Reader

1. Tim and Anne Evans, *TOGETHER: Reclaiming Co-Leadership in Marriage* (Colorado Springs, CO: REAL LIFE Ministries, 2014). Available at Amazon.com.
2. Tim and Anne Evans, *NAKED: Reclaiming Sexual Intimacy in Marriage* (Colorado Springs, CO: REAL LIFE Ministries, 2017). Available at Amazon.com.
3. Acts 16:14

Foreword

1. Gilbert Bilezikian, Th.D., *Community 101: Reclaiming the Local Church as Community of Oneness* (Grand Rapids, Michigan: Zondervan, 1997) 15.

Introduction

1. *Urban Dictionary*, s.v. "soulgasm."

Chapter 1: SOUL *what?*

1. Genesis 1:27
2. 1 Thessalonians 5:23
3. John 11:35
4. Matthew 21:13 NIV
5. Ephesians 4:26 ESV
6. Matthew 26:39
7. Mark 1:11
8. Matthew 8:10
9. Matthew 14:14
10. Matthew 19:14
11. Genesis 1:27
12. Genesis 3:8
13. Genesis 2:24
14. Genesis 2:25
15. Genesis 1:31
16. Frederick Buechner, *The Remarkable Ordinary,* quoting from the back cover (Grand Rapids, Michigan: Zondervan, 2017).

17. We first heard this definition of intimacy in a Wheaton course with Dr. Gilbert Bilezikian, Spring 1987.
18. 1 Thessalonians 5:23
19. Genesis 2:24
20. 1 Corinthians 7:28
21. The concept of Larger Story/smaller story living is adapted from the teaching and writings of John Eldredge and Dan B. Allender, PhD.

Chapter 2: Understanding Your Family of Origin Influences

1. *Encarta Dictionary*, s.v. "legacy."
2. 2 Corinthians 5:17 NLT
3. James 1:5

Chapter 3: Celebrating Your Spouse's Uniqueness

1. 1 Corinthians 7:28 NIV
2. Matthew 19:5
3. Genesis 2:25
4. Genesis 2:24 KJV
5. 1 Timothy 4:16
6. Genesis 1:27
7. Proverbs 11:14
8. Genesis 2:25
9. For more information, visit https://spiritualgiftstest.com/spiritual-gifts-test-adult-version/.
10. Peter Wagner, *Your Spiritual Gifts Can Help Your Church Grow* (Ventura, CA: Regal, 1979), 44.
11. For more information visit http://www.onlinediscprofile.com/.
12. For more information visit http://www.tjta.com/abouttjta.htm.
13. Gary Chapman, *The Five Love Languages* (Chicago: Northfield, 1992).
14. John 13:34-35
15. Genesis 1:27
16. Genesis 1:28
17. *TOGETHER: Reclaiming Co-Leadership in Marriage* by Tim and Anne Evans unpacks God's creational marriage design.

Chapter 4: Distinguishing Between Roles and Functions

1. Genesis 2:24
2. Genesis 1:28
3. Matthew 22:37-40
4. Matthew 23:11 NIV
5. Genesis 1:26

6. Christians for Biblical Equality (CBE) website at www.cbeinternational.org.
7. Matthew 3:2
8. Matthew 11:11 NIV
9. Genesis 2:18
10. Exodus 15:3
11. *Merriam-Webster Dictionary*, s.v. "machismo."
12. Hosea 11:9; Numbers 23:19
13. John 4:24 KJV
14. Exodus 15:3
15. 2 Corinthians 1:3-5
16. 1 Thessalonians 2:7-8
17. Matthew 11:29
18. Genesis 1:27
19. Matthew 4:19

Chapter 5: Living Out Love and Respect

1. Dr. Emerson Eggerichs, *Love and Respect* (Nashville, TN: Thomas Nelson, 2004). Also, *Love and Respect* conferences with Dr. Emerson and Sarah Eggerichs.
2. Ephesians 5:33
3. This updated story was originally shared in *TOGETHER: Reclaiming Co-Leadership in Marriage*, chapter 10.
4. Ephesians 5:33
5. Matthew 22:37-40
6. 1 Corinthians 12:31 NIV
7. 1 Corinthians 13:13 NIV
8. Hebrews 13:4
9. John 21:15-17
10. Christians for Biblical Equality (CBE) website at www.cbeinternational.org.
11. 1 Peter 5:5
12. 1 Corinthians 13:11
13. Genesis 2:24
14. Jeremiah 9:8

Chapter 6: Steps of Intimacy

1. Genesis 2:25
2. Desmond Morris, *Intimate Behavior* (New York: Kodansha America, 1971).
3. Romans 16:16; 2 Corinthians 13:12
4. Joshua Harris, *I Kissed Dating Goodbye* (Colorado Springs, CO: Multnomah Books, 1997).
5. Adelle M. Banks, "With High Premarital Sex and Abortion Rates, Evangelicals Say It's Time to Talk about Sex," *Huffington Post* online, April 23, 2012 (https://m.huffpost.com/us/entry/1443062).
6. Genesis 2:24

Chapter 7: SOUL*gasm* Sex

1. A similar version of this material was also published in *NAKED: Reclaiming Sexual Intimacy in Marriage*.
2. Genesis 1:26
3. Colossians 3:17
4. Genesis 1:28
5. Matthew 22:37-40
6. Song of Solomon 5:1
7. 2 Samuel 12:24
8. 1 Corinthians 7:3-5
9. *Merriam-Webster Dictionary*, s.v. "duty."
10. Matthew 22:37-40
11. Colossians 3:17
12. 1 Corinthians 7:3-5
13. 1 Corinthians 7:5
14. Hebrews 13:4 ESV
15. *Encarta Dictionary*, s.v. "honor."
16. *Encarta Dictionary*, s.v. "defiled."
17. Bob Dylan, "The Times They Are a-Changin'," Columbia Records, 1964.
18. Genesis 3:16
19. Genesis 1:27
20. Genesis 1:28
21. Genesis 2:24
22. Genesis 2:25
23. Christians for Biblical Equality (CBE) website at www.cbeinternational.org.
24. Ephesians 5:21
25. Ephesians 4:12 NLT
26. Tim and Anne Evans, *NAKED: Reclaiming Sexual Intimacy in Marriage*, *NAKED Companion Journal*, and *NAKED Sexual Agreement* (Colorado Springs, CO: REAL LIFE Ministries, 2017). Available at Amazon.com.

Chapter 8: Sowing Negativity and Reaping Negativity

1. Galatians 6:7
2. Galatians 6:7
3. Genesis 2:24-25
4. 1 Timothy 4:16
5. Matthew 7:3-5
6. 1 Corinthians 7:28

Chapter 9: Unrighteous Judging

1. https://www.quora.com/How-many-people-in-the-US-buy-lottery-tickets-every-year.

2. 1 Corinthians 2:15
3. Matthew 7:1-2 NIV
4. Romans 2:1
5. Ephesians 6:12 NKJV
6. 1 Samuel 16:7
7. Acts 15:8
8. 1 Corinthians 2:15
9. 2 Corinthians 10:5
10. James 1:5
11. Psalm 44:21
12. Philippians 4:8
13. 1 Timothy 4:16
14. Matthew 19:8
15. John 8:7-11
16. 1 Corinthians 6:18
17. Matthew 7:1 NIV
18. Romans 2:1-2
19. Philippians 4:8 TLB

Chapter 10: Handling Offenses Poorly

1. Proverbs 19:11 NIV
2. Philippians 2:3
3. Matthew 12:34
4. Matthew 12:34
5. James 3
6. Proverbs 4:23 NIV
7. Matthew 12:34
8. 1 Samuel 16:7

Chapter 11: Failing to Honor Parents

1. Deuteronomy 5:16
2. Ephesians 6:4 NIV
3. Deuteronomy 5:16
4. Deuteronomy 5:16

Chapter 12: Choosing Pride Over Humility

1. 2 Chronicles 1:7-12 NIV
2. Matthew 23:12
3. 1 Peter 5:5
4. Andrew Murray, *Humility* (Ada, MI: Bethany House Publishers, 2001). Originally published in 1895, there are several republished versions available online.
5. Dr. C. Peter Wagner, *Humility* (Bloomington, MN: Chosen Books, 2002).
6. 2 Chronicles 1:7-12 NIV
7. Matthew 23:12

8. 1 Peter 5:5
9. Proverbs 9:10
10. 1 Peter 5:5

Chapter 13: Stuck in Overdrive—the Fast Pace of Life

1. Tom Stella, spiritual director, in a conversation in Colorado Springs, Colorado, with Tim, fall 2017.
2. Tim and Anne encourage readers to visit *AXIS Ministry* (https://axis.org/) and sign up for *The Cultural Translator*. You will receive regular emails that equip you to understand and deal with culturally relevant topics, with wisdom and grace.
3. John Eldredge, RANSOMED HEART newsletter, March 2018 (www. RANSOMEDHEART.com).
4. The shame-fear-control-rebellion-rejection concept is adapted from the teaching and writings of Dr. Chester and Betsy Kylstra, *Restoring the Foundations* (www. restoringthefoundations.org). Also, for further information, Dr. Brené Brown is considered an expert on shame, vulnerability, worthiness, and courage (http:// brenebrown.com).

Chapter 14: The Importance of Leaving a Legacy

1. Genesis 2:24; Matthew 19:5
2. 1 Timothy 4:16
3. 1 Corinthians 13:9
4. Genesis 2:25
5. Hebrews 12:25
6. 2 Corinthians 10:5 NIV
7. James 1:5 NIV
8. Proverbs 29:18
9. Genesis 1:27
10. Matthew 12:34 NIV
11. Frederick Buechner, *The Remarkable Ordinary*, (Grand Rapids, Michigan: Zondervan, 2017) 114.
12. James 4:6
13. Philippians 4:7 ESV
14. 1 Peter 5:5
15. 1 Peter 3:15 NIV
16. Romans 1:16
17. Tim and Anne Evans, *NAKED: Reclaiming Sexual Intimacy in Marriage* (Colorado Springs, CO: REAL LIFE Ministries, 2017) 233.
18. Matthew 6:33 ESV

Chapter 15: What's the "Secret Ingredient" in Marriage?

1. 1 Corinthians 7:28

2. 1 Corinthians 13:11 NIV

Epilogue

1. Romans 8:38-39
2. John 3:16
3. Proverbs 29:18 KJV
4. Genesis 1:26-27
5. Acts 18:26
6. Genesis 2:24
7. Genesis 2:25
8. 1 Peter 1:3
9. Ephesians 4:12 NLT
10. Genesis 2:24
11. Christians for Biblical Equality (CBE) website at www.cbeinternational.org.
12. Genesis 2:25

Appendix A: Co-Leadership in Marriage

1. Tim and Anne Evans, *TOGETHER: Reclaiming Co-Leadership in Marriage* (Colorado Springs, CO: REAL LIFE Ministries, 2014). Available at Amazon.com.
2. Genesis 1:26
3. Genesis 1:28
4. Genesis 3:16
5. Gilbert Bilezikian, Th.D., *Beyond Sex Roles*, 3rd edition (Grand Rapids, MI: Baker Academic, 2006), 99-100.
6. Luke 19:10 KJV

Appendix B: I.O.T.L.—*Inquire of the Lord*

1. 2 Corinthians 10:5 NIV
2. Judges 20:23; Judges 20:27; 1 Samuel 23:2,4; 2 Samuel 5:23; 1 Chronicles 14:10
3. 1 Corinthians 6:19; Romans 8:9; 1 Corinthians 3:16
4. 2 Corinthians 10:5 NIV
5. Proverbs 3:5-6
6. James 1:5

Appendix C: The **Traffic Light Principle**

1. Proverbs 3:5-6
2. James 1:5
3. James 1:5 NIV
4. Hebrews 12:25
5. Proverbs 11:14
6. James 4:2
7. Proverbs 3:4-6 TLB

8. Genesis 2:24
9. Genesis 2:25

Appendix D: Listening to God

1. Hebrews 12:25
2. Tim and Anne Evans, *TOGETHER: Reclaiming Co-Leadership in Marriage* (Colorado Springs, CO: REAL LIFE Ministries, 2014) 112-115.
3. Philippians 4:6
4. 2 Corinthians 10:5
5. 1 Corinthians 2:15
6. James 1:5 NIV
7. Proverbs 11:14
8. Colossians 3:17
9. Matthew 6:33
10. 1 Thessalonians 5:16-18
11. Philippians 4:7 ESV
12. Genesis 1-2
13. Luke 18:29-30
14. Ephesians 4:1 ESV
15. 2 Timothy 1:9
16. 1 Samuel 16:7
17. Luke 6:45
18. Matthew 22:37-40

Appendix E: Core Real Life Values

1. Our next book in our REAL LIFE Marriage Series is titled *BEST Marriage Now!* It includes a number of core life-giving marriage principles. Available soon.
2. Genesis 1:26-27
3. Genesis 1:27
4. Hosea 11:9; Numbers 23:19; 1 Samuel 15:29
5. 1 Thessalonians 5:23
6. Genesis 1:26,28
7. Genesis 1:26
8. Genesis 1:28
9. The concept of Larger Story/smaller story living is adapted from the teaching and writings of John Eldredge and Dan B. Allender, PhD.

REAL LIFE MARRIAGE SERIES

By Tim + Anne Evans

+ BOOK SET #1

TOGETHER: Reclaiming Co-Leadership in Marriage

TOGETHER Companion Journal

+ BOOK SET #2

NAKED: Reclaiming Sexual Intimacy in Marriage

NAKED Companion Journal

NAKED Sexual Agreement

+ BOOK SET #3

SOUL*gasm*: Caring for Your Soul and the Soul of Your Marriage

SOUL*gasm* Companion Journal

+ BOOK SET #4 *(coming soon)*

BEST Marriage NOW!

BEST Marriage NOW! Companion Journal

REAL LIFE Books and Companion Journals can be purchased at Amazon.com

ADDITIONAL REAL LIFE MARRIAGE RESOURCES AVAILABLE ON AMAZON.

NAKED

Reclaiming **Sexual Intimacy** in Marriage

tim+anne evans

NAKED
COMPANION JOURNAL

Reclaiming **Sexual Intimacy** in Marriage

anne+tim evans

NAKED
SEXUAL AGREEMENT

Advancing in **Intimacy** with your Spouse

anne+tim evans

SOULgasm
Caring for Your **Soul** and the **Soul** of Your Marriage

anne+tim evans

SOULgasm
COMPANION JOURNAL

Caring for Your **Soul** and the **Soul** of Your Marriage

anne+tim evans

SOUL*gasm*

Caring for Your **Soul** and the **Soul** of Your Marriage

Made in the USA
Lexington, KY
20 September 2018